Language, Frogs and Savants

To Zachary and Joshua
Unalloyed Joy

Language, Frogs and Savants

More Linguistic Problems, Puzzles and Polemics

Neil Smith

Blackwell
Publishing

BLACKWELL PUBLISHING
350 Main Street, Malden, MA 02148-5020, USA
9600 Garsington Road, Oxford OX4 2DQ, UK
550 Swanston Street, Carlton, Victoria 3053, Australia

First published 2005 by Blackwell Publishing Ltd

1   2005

Library of Congress Cataloging-in-Publication Data

Smith, N. V. (Neilson Voyne)
    Language, frogs, and savants : more linguistic problems, puzzles, and polemics / Neil Smith.
        p. cm.
    Includes bibliographical references and index.
    ISBN-13: 978-1-4051-3037-0 (hard cover : alk. paper)
    ISBN-10: 1-4051-3037-7 (hard cover : alk. paper)
    ISBN-13: 978-1-4051-3038-7 (pbk. : alk paper)
    ISBN-10: 1-4051-3038-5 (pbk. : alk. paper)
    1. Language and languages.   2. Linguistics.   I. Title.
    P107 .S65 2005
    400—dc22

                                                        2005009256

A catalogue record for this title is available from the British Library.

Set in 10.5/13pt Meridien
by Graphicraft Limited, Hong Kong
Printed and bound in India
by Replika Press Ltd

The publisher's policy is to use permanent paper from mills that operate a sustainable forestry policy, and which has been manufactured from pulp processed using acid-free and elementary chlorine-free practices. Furthermore, the publisher ensures that the text paper and cover board used have met acceptable environmental accreditation standards.

For further information on
Blackwell Publishing, visit our website:
www.blackwellpublishing.com

Contents

Part III Core Concerns 101

Preface

A craving for understanding.

Language holds a fascination for everyone. For some it can become an obsession, and for a privileged few it can be the basis for making a living. As a professional linguist all my life I have been able to indulge my obsession at the tax-payers' expense, and in this collection of essays I want to repay some of the accumulated debt. I would like to share the fun, enlighten the lay reader, and simultaneously perhaps remove some of the misapprehensions of psychologists, neurologists, and other members of the cognitive science community who are professionally involved with language.

The essays that follow consist partly of revised and updated versions of columns that appeared in the electronic journal *Glot International*, and partly of lectures and reviews that have either not been previously published or have been radically changed. They were initially addressed to an audience with some basic expertise in linguistics. As this cannot be expected of everyone reading this collection, and as I wish to make the essays as accessible as possible, I have provided a lengthy introduction to one version of current linguistics: that associated most closely with the work of Noam Chomsky. I have also compiled a glossary in which I have defined and exemplified any terms that may be unfamiliar or used in ways that differ from their normal non-linguistic usage.

As in my previous collection, *Language, Bananas and Bonobos*, the essays fall into three categories, of Problems, Puzzles and Polemics. As before, all of them address issues which are simultaneously problematic, puzzling or polemical in one way or another, so I have ordered them not under those headings but into three different groups. The first, 'Language in the Limit', deals with cases which are in some way or other exceptional: they deal with the remarkable talents of savants, with the complexities of signed languages, with the insights and foibles of those on the periphery of formal studies of language, from Shakespeare's rhetorical devices to etymology and linguistic censorship. This is followed by a genetic interlude, 'Language in the Genes', discussing the fashionable preoccupation with innateness and the genetic determination of the language faculty. The final group, 'Core Concerns', turns to issues which are, perhaps surprisingly, more central to current theoretical linguistics: the definition of *the*, the mispronunciations of two-year-olds, and the use of statistics. The grouping is not mandatory, and the essays can be read in any order. Most of them should be accessible to anyone prepared to go slowly and think about the examples, though I have sometimes included technicalities for my colleagues.

Linguistics is ultimately preoccupied with specifying what it means to 'know a language', and providing explanations for how this knowledge is possible. Our mastery of language can seem deceptively straightforward until we try to make explicit what precisely an infant exposed to English or any other language has to master before it counts as a speaker of that language, or what precisely has been lost by someone who has had a stroke. An illustration of a minute fraction of what we know can be given with examples of words and sentences about which we have particular intuitions, that we can judge as well- or ill-formed, or ambiguous. Listening to the radio this morning I heard a minister declare that 'the government promised not to force people to work until they were seventy'. I first took this to mean that the government would wait until we were seventy before forcing us to work, and only a second or two later came up with the less cynical interpretation that working until we were seventy was something the government would not force us to do. Being potentially aware of both these possibilities is part of what it means to know English. Take an even simpler, and less loaded, example: a linguist might say either *I am studying word order in Arabic* or *I am studying the word order of Arabic*, but it would be odd to say either *I am studying the word order in Arabic* or *I am studying word order of Arabic*. For the moment it doesn't matter precisely why this should be the case; what is important is that you appreciate that it is indeed true – that you had this knowledge of English despite the fact that (I suspect) you have never been taught it or even noticed it before. After having had it pointed out, you may even think that it is entirely trivial, but the subtlety of such knowledge can reveal interesting properties of the human mind. Our knowledge of language includes an infinite and dazzling array of such facts, a few of which will be discussed in more detail below. The delicacy and depth of such judgements means that, although I have tried to make the chapters of this book user-friendly, every example needs to be thought about, so that – if you disagree with what I write – you can disagree with me constructively rather than just from a feeling of contrariness.

I am grateful to a number of people: to Lisa Cheng and Rint Sybesma, who invited me to write the columns for *Glot International* that provide the basis for many of these chapters; to colleagues and friends, who have goaded or inspired me; to Annabel Cormack, Ann Law and Phoevos Panagiotidis, who have provided me with sage comment on, and penetrating criticism of, much of what follows.

As always, my deepest debt is to my family – from A to Z.

Introduction: What Everyone Should Know about Language and Linguistics

They have been at a great feast of languages and stolen the scraps.
William Shakespeare, *Love's Labour's Lost*

Why bother with linguistics?

We all know (at least) one language that we use effortlessly to get around in the world: to communicate with our family and friends, to earn our living, even to interact with disembodied voices over the telephone. So why do we need to care about the etymology of 'nice' or 'hysteria', or learn about deponent verbs and subordinate clauses, or agonize over the pronunciation of 'controversy'? Such matters only breed confusion. So what's the point?

The answer comes in several steps. To begin with, we need to disabuse people: etymology, notions of correctness, and the arcane vocabulary of traditional grammatical description are not what linguistics is about. Rather, it is concerned with three things: discovering precisely what it means to 'know a language'; providing techniques for describing this knowledge; and explaining why our knowledge takes the form it does.

These concerns may seem too obvious to need discussing, but the complexity of our knowledge of language becomes strikingly apparent when we see someone lose their language after an accident, or when we observe a young child that is still acquiring the ability that we deploy so easily. To understand this we need a theory, and that is what linguistics provides.

I   The Meaning of 'Language'

That linguistics is 'the scientific study of language' has become a cliché, but what it means to be 'scientific' may not always be obvious, and what people mean when they use the word 'language' varies from occasion to occasion. Consideration of what is involved in being scientific is deferred till section V; for now it suffices to observe that only a few aspects of language have been illuminated by theoretical (scientific) linguistics, so there are many areas where it has little, if anything, helpful to say. The situation is akin to that in biology, viewed as the science of living things. Despite their importance to us, biology has nothing to say about the definition of pets; similarly, despite their relevance to us, linguistics has nothing to say about the definition of dialects.

In everyday usage, 'language' is used differently depending on whether it is construed as a property of the individual, of society, of the species, or as an autonomous entity in the world. Linguists working in the tradition of 'generative' grammar, the framework which has dominated linguistics for the last fifty years, argue that an 'individual' approach to language is logically prior to any other, but, in principle, we have the possible domains in (1), each suggesting different kinds of question:

1.   Language and the Individual
     Language and the Brain
     Language and Society
     Language and the Species
     Language and Literature
     Language and the World

Looking at 'Language and the Individual', the central question raised is 'what constitutes our 'knowledge of language'? What properties or attributes does one have to have to be correctly described as a speaker of English, or Burmese, or any other 'natural language' – the term linguists use to refer to languages naturally acquired and spoken by humans, as opposed to the 'artificial' languages of logic or computing? An extension of this question is how and where knowledge of language is represented in the brain, and what mechanisms need to be postulated to enable us to account for our use of this knowledge. Neurolinguistics is currently an area of remarkable growth, supported by technological advances in imaging that have opened many new horizons.

Under 'Language and Society', sociolinguists raise questions like 'What are the social variants (class, age, gender, power) which determine, or correlate with, the use of particular forms of the language?' A woman might use some pronunciations or grammatical constructions with statistically significantly greater frequency than a man of the same age, or a female of a different generation. For the world's multilingual majority, social considerations may even determine which language is used in specific situations. A Swiss from Graubünden might use Romansh at home, Swiss German at work, and High German at a conference.

Looking at 'Language and the Species', we might be preoccupied with the puzzle that all human children learn their first language with seeming effortlessness, whilst the young of other species, however intelligent, show minimal such ability. Linguists, and researchers in related fields, investigate not only whether this claim to uniqueness is indeed true but, if it is, how the faculty evolved. A corollary which emerges from this species orientation is the surprising similarity of all languages when we look a little below the surface. To a dispassionate Martian all languages would look much the same. We may have difficulty understanding Chinese or even interacting with our neighbours across the Channel, but there is a sense in which we all speak 'human'; all languages are cut from the same cloth.

When we turn to the relation between Language and Literature, we confront several issues: 'What is literary form?'; that is, what are the linguistic properties that make something a novel or a novella, a sonnet or an epic? How are literary effects achieved? What are the linguistic characteristics of a particular style or author that enable us to distinguish Milton from Shakespeare or, closer to home, a genuine confession from a fabrication? It is notorious that the confession which resulted in Timothy Evans being hanged in 1950 (for one of the 10 Rillington Place murders) was probably concocted by the police: stylistic analysis might have saved his life.

Looking at 'Language and the World' raises issues of at least three different kinds. First, assuming the validity of the claim that we can study an individual's knowledge of language, we need to investigate how language relates to things outside the head. That the word 'London' refers to the capital of the UK is innocuous enough as an informal claim, but it raises interesting, and vexed, philosophical questions. The debate revolves around disagreement about the status of language as an 'internal' property of an individual, rather than as an 'external' entity with independent existence. The external notion of language is presupposed by those who write irate letters to the press. Is it incorrect to split infinitives? Is it wrong to say (or worse, write) 'He gave it to John and I'? Can 'hysterical' really be used of men, who don't have the womb that provides its etymology from Greek? More generally, is our language becoming degenerate, either because of the sloppiness of modern youth, or the pernicious influence of text messaging, or the role of multi-culturalism? The third issue is in many ways the most obvious and the most puzzling: why are there so many languages? If we all speak 'human', why does it have so many dialects?

The generativist claim that study of the individual's knowledge of language must be the first or exclusive focus of a scientific linguistics is controversial; that it is a possible, indeed necessary, focus is not seriously in doubt. This individualistic claim implies that linguistics is a branch of psychology, ultimately of biology, rather than, say, of sociology. This is not to deny that there are interesting domains of knowledge that take the social conditions of language use as their central focus; it is rather to claim that there is a psychological enterprise which looks at one branch of human cognition and which lends itself to rigorous investigation and, moreover, that it is logically prior to looking at the exploitation of this knowledge in society. This focus on knowledge is highlighted in the claim that the subject of linguistics is 'I-language', rather than 'E-language', where the 'I' stand for *i*nternal to a particular *i*ndividual, and 'E' stands for *e*xternal (to the mind of the individual). This orientation implies that the descriptions that linguists devise are 'psychologically real', where this is not a claim about psychological experimentation or the kind of evidence used in formulating particular linguistic hypotheses; it is simply the claim that we are investigating the human mind and that current theory is the closest approximation to the truth that we have.

The mind is ultimately a product of the brain (and other systems), and evidence about the mental can sometimes be gleaned from studies of the neural. In general, however, linguists remain agnostic about the details of the relation between the mind and the brain (frequently referring simply to the 'mind/brain'). That is, we devise theories of a sub-part of human knowledge, but whether that knowledge is localized in the temporal lobe of the left hemisphere, or is distributed throughout the brain, or whatever, is less important. This is not because of lack of interest, but simply because – at present – theories of neural structure are too embryonic to cast much light on linguistic generalizations. For example, different languages allow different word orders, so that Japanese puts the verb at the end of the sentence and English puts it in the middle: where English has *Marvin opened the door*, with the order Subject Verb Object (SVO), Japanese has *Marvin door opened*, with the order Subject Object Verb (SOV). Linguistic theory must provide the means for describing and ultimately explaining this fact, but at present we have no inkling of how the difference between a Japanese and an English speaker might be neurally implemented, so the neurological structure of (this bit of) the language faculty is still largely a closed book. What neurological insight we do have comes mainly from two directions: pathology and imaging. If it turns out consistently to be the case that a blow to the left hemisphere causes loss of language whereas a blow to the right does not, it is a reasonably safe assumption that the left hemisphere is the seat of language. So much is not in dispute, and the finding is corroborated by imaging studies that can pinpoint neural activity while subjects are undertaking specific linguistic tasks, but this is still a far cry from knowing what brain mechanism underlies the difference between SVO and SOV word order.

II Knowledge of Language

What do you have to know to count as a 'speaker' of a language? If you say you speak English, it implies that you understand English as well. The point may seem obvious, but knowing a language is neutral as between speaking and hearing; both activities draw on the same fund of knowledge. There is no known illness or accident which leaves you able to speak only English and understand only Portuguese, for instance. This is not to deny that you may be better at talking than listening; or that you may suffer brain damage that leaves you unable to speak while you remain perfectly able to understand. A particularly poignant example of this is provided by Bauby's (1997) autobiographical account of 'locked-in' syndrome, where a stroke left the author speechless, but with his language and his ability to understand intact. He managed to write the book by controlling one eye-lid, which allowed him to indicate letters of the alphabet presented in sequence to him. In normal, non-pathological, cases, however, your ability to *utter* (2a):

2a.   Giraffes have long necks
  b.   Giraffes have necks long

involves the same ability that enables you to *understand* (2a), and also to judge that someone who mistakenly says (2b) has got it wrong. The implication of this observation is that the primary focus of linguistics is on characterizing this neutral knowledge, rather than the mechanisms of speaking, hearing and judging that are parasitic on it. In other words linguistics is (largely) about one form of cognition, and only secondarily about the deployment of that cognitive ability. In the standard terminology this is known as the 'competence–performance' distinction. Your knowledge of language (your competence) underlies your ability to speak, to understand and to give judgements of well- or ill-formedness (your performance). You may be knocked unconscious and be temporarily unable to speak or understand, but your knowledge typically remains intact – you have competence with no ability for performance. The converse situation, in which you could perform in the absence of any competence, does not occur, though it may characterize the 'linguistic' capabilities of the average parrot, which may be able to utter entertaining sentences of what sounds like English, but presumably without the knowledge of English grammar that underlies our abilities.[1]

To count as a speaker of English you need first to know a large number of words: not just nouns, verbs and adjectives – words like *cat* and *go* and *pretty*, whose meaning is relatively transparent – but items like *the*, *under*, and *however*, whose meaning and use are less easy to specify. Of course, not everyone has the same vocabulary:

I may know technical terms in linguistics that you are ignorant of, and you may be familiar with words pertaining to reggae or arachnology that I don't know, but if either of us were ignorant of words like *mother* or *and*, people might be justifiably reluctant to classify us as speakers of English.

As well as knowing the words of a language, you need to know what to do with those words – you need to know the grammar. Our knowledge of language falls into two compartments – the vocabulary (or 'lexicon') and the 'computations' we can carry out using that vocabulary. This computational system, comprising syntax and morphology, is surprisingly complex, as should become clear as we look at more and more sentences. It even enables us to produce baroque examples like Chomsky's (1995a:88) *Who do you wonder whether John said solved the problem?* which are of such marginal acceptability that citing them may strain the tolerance of outsiders. Importantly, however, this marginal status may itself provide crucial evidence for or against some theoretical claim concerning our knowledge, so such examples cannot be lightly dismissed. Henceforth I shall assume that you and I have the same I-language, abstracting away from differences in vocabulary and grammar. Fortunately, it's enough for present purposes to look at the more basic, but nonetheless rich and surprising, knowledge we have of words as simple as *be* and *the*, which can be used to illustrate a wide range of things you know, even if you weren't previously aware of knowing them.

It's self-evident that *is* and *have* mean different things, as shown in (3), but sometimes they seem to be used interchangeably as in (4):

3a.   Tom is a problem
  b.   Tom has a problem

4a.   Tim is yet to win the Booker prize
  b.   Tim has yet to win the Booker prize

How is it that something as basic as *is* can sometimes get the same interpretation as *has* and sometimes a different one? Or consider the so-called definite article (*the*), which is often said to mark the distinction between entities which are already familiar and those which are new, as in (5a) and (5b) respectively:

5a.   My friend likes the penguins
 b.   My friend likes penguins

But this characterization is not adequate to account for the rather macabre effects found in the newspaper report in (6b) beside the relatively unexceptionable (6a):

6a.   The woman had lived with the dead man for two years
 b.   The woman had lived with a dead man for two years

Still less can it account for the fact (see chapter 16 below) that on occasion the presence or absence of *the* seems to indicate the difference between subject and object, as in (7):

7a.   This man is in charge of my brother
 b.   This man is in the charge of my brother

In (7a) *this man* has control of *my brother*; in (7b) *my brother* has control of *this man*. So what does *the* really mean? Does it even make sense to ask such a question?

Take a more complex example: the word *last* is multiply ambiguous: apart from its use as a noun (the cobbler's *last*) or a verb (the party *lasted* all night), it can function as an adjective meaning either 'final' or 'previous', as illustrated in (8):

8a.   This is your last chance
 b.   Your last example surprised me

This ambiguity can result in dialogues which have strikingly different interpretations, as in the alternatives in (9):

9.   Q   'What were you doing in Paris?'
 A1   'Oh, I was collecting material for my last book'
 A2   'Oh, I'm collecting material for my last book'

Answer 1 is itself ambiguous, with either meaning possible for *last* (though 'previous' is the more easily accessible); answer 2 has only the interpretation that the book under discussion is planned to be the final one I write. The difference must be attributable to the contrast between the past and the present tense, as that is the only way the sentences differ, but it's not obvious why sentences should be ambiguous or not depending on the tense they contain.

Linguists thrive on such ambiguity, as it regularly provides evidence for structural differences that may not be otherwise apparent. A simple example is provided by the inscrutable notice outside our local school, given in (10):

10. This school accepts girls and boys under six

Whether the school accepts girls of any age but only small boys, or no children over six, is indeterminate without more information. As we shall see in section III, (10) has two quite different syntactic structures corresponding to the two meanings. Similarly the fact that (11) has a number of different interpretations can give us clues as to how to analyse the various possibilities:

11. My son has grown another foot

If my son has become taller, the example is parallel to (12a); if he is a freak or a remarkably successful gardener, there are other possibilities, as shown in (12b) and (12c), suggesting that *another foot* in (11) may be correctly analysed either as a 'measure phrase' or as a 'direct object':

12a. He has grown by another foot
 b. He has grown a third foot
 c. Another foot has been grown (in this flower-pot).

Such differences of interpretation make the complexity of our knowledge apparent, but unambiguous examples can be just as illuminating and can simultaneously provide evidence against the traditional philosophical claim that meaning can be adequately treated in terms of truth. Thus, we know that (13):

13. My first wife gave me this watch

suggests rather strongly that I have been married more than once, but I can utter it truthfully despite having been married only once: my only wife is presumably my first wife. The example is misleading, not false, and so implies that there is much more to meaning than mere truth. As shown by Chomsky's (1957) famous *Colorless green ideas sleep furiously*, structure and meaning (syntax and semantics) can dissociate, so we also know that, despite being initially plausible and syntactically unexceptionable, (14) is meaningless:

14.   More people have visited Moscow than I have

All the preceding examples illustrate both our knowledge of vocabulary and how it interacts with (syntactic) structure. The responsibility of linguistics is to describe the full range of such facts, not just for English, but for all human languages. Then, in virtue of its scientific pretensions, it has to (attempt to) explain why these facts rather than any others are the ones that occur – again both in English and in other languages. To do justice to the richness of what we know, it is necessary to distinguish not just the lexicon and the computational system, but to differentiate among syntax, semantics, morphology, phonology and phonetics, and to relate this knowledge to pragmatics – how we interpret utterances in context.

Take our knowledge of morphology, the internal structure of words. We know that *thick, thicker, thickest* and *thicken* are all words of English, but that there is no *thinnen* to accompany *thin, thinner, thinnest*. We know that *thick* relates to *thicken* and that *rich* relates to *enrich*, whereas *richen* is slightly odd, and *enthick* is impossible.[2] This knowledge can't just be a result of our never having heard *thinnen* or *enthick* before; you may never have heard *texted* before, as in 'I've just texted an urgent message to Fred', but you know that that **is** possible.[3] As linguists, we may also know that some languages, such as Vietnamese, have almost no morphology: words in this language have none of the internal structure characteristic of affix-rich items like *indecisiveness* or *rearranged*. On the other hand, some (polysynthetic) languages, such as Inuktitut (Eskimo) or Mohawk, pile one affix on top of another so that words are often strikingly complex, and correspond to whole sentences in English. Baker (2001b:87) gives the one-word Mohawk example in (15) with the meaning 'He made the thing that one puts on one's body ugly for her':

15.   Washakotya'tawitsherahetkvhta'se'

Our knowledge of phonology, the sound structure of language, is equally rich. We know that *past, spat* and *stap* are possible words of English, indeed they all exist; that *stip* and *stup* are also possible words, even though they happen not to exist; but that *satp*, *ptas* and *tpas* are not even possible words. Apart from having knowledge of this kind about the segmental make-up of words, we also have knowledge of 'supra-segmentals': that *phótograph* is stressed on the first syllable, *photógrapher* on the second, and *photográphic* on the third. Two points need to be made: first, we 'know' this in the sense that we produce the correct pronunciations on demand, and recognize that deviations from these pronunciations are slips of the tongue or the mistakes of foreign learners; that is, knowledge of language need not be immediately available to conscious introspection. Second, the characterization in terms of 'first', 'second' and 'third' syllable is actually not the correct theoretical characterization of our knowledge. As we shall see below, rules of grammar (including phonology) cannot count.

We know more. In an example like (5a) above, *My friend likes the penguins*, we have to account for the pronunciation of *the* before the initial 'p' of *penguins*: a pronunciation rather different from that of the same lexical item *the* when it occurs before a vowel, as in *My friend likes the otters*. Knowledge of this kind is supplemented by phonetic knowledge which is even harder to bring to consciousness: that the 't' in *photographer* is aspirated, but the 't' in *photograph* is not; that the 'r' in *grime* is voiced, but that in *prime* is slightly devoiced; that the vowel is longer in *wed* than in *wet*. Such facts belong to the domain of phonetics, the field which deals with the sound properties of language in general, rather than the sound structure of a particular language.

Our phonological knowledge is not self-contained, but may interact in complex ways with our knowledge of the rest of the grammar. We know that (16a) has an alternative pronunciation of the kind given in (16b), where *is* is 'contracted' to *'s*, but that (17a) cannot be matched by the impossible (17b) (as indicated by the asterisk), despite the apparent similarity of the examples:

16a. The prime minister is a war criminal
  b. The prime minister's a war criminal

17a. The president is a war criminal and the prime minister is too
  b. *The president is a war criminal and the prime minister's too

An understanding of such asymmetries requires investigation of the relation between syntactic and phonological processes, and relies on an analysis of 'empty categories' (see chapter 15 below): entities that have syntactic and semantic properties but are silent.

In addition to phonology and morphology, we need to account for the (semantic) fact that sentences have meaning. The examples in (18) exploit most of the same words but their meanings are radically different:

18a.   My friend likes the penguins
  b.   The penguins like my friend
  c.   My friend doesn't like the penguins

Moreover, the semantics is 'compositional' – except for idioms, the meaning of a sentence is a function of the meaning of its parts, and their syntactic configuration. The meaning difference between (18a) and (18b) is dependent on which item is subject and which object, notions that can be defined syntactically. In fact, life is a little more complicated than that, as the semantic interpretation of 'subject' is not uniform, and we need to advert to 'thematic relations' involving ideas of agentivity and patienthood, as shown by the minimal pair in (19):

19a.   John undertook the surgery reluctantly
  b.   John underwent the surgery reluctantly

John is the subject in both sentences, but is the agent (the surgeon) in the former, and the patient (in both senses) in the latter. These relations are internal to a single sentence, but we also need to capture the relations between (the meanings of) different sentences. Here, there are two possibilities: those relations which depend on the meaning of individual words, and those relations which are purely sentential in that they are largely independent of particular lexical items. An example of the former is illustrated by (20):

20a.   Mozart persuaded da Ponte to write a libretto
  b.   Da Ponte intended to write something

where (20b) follows, in virtue of the meaning of *persuade*, from (20a). An example of the latter is provided by pairs such as (21) where, if (21a) is true, then it must necessarily be the case that (21b) is also true:[4]

21a. Torture is immoral and should be illegal
  b. Torture is immoral

In the next section I will outline some of the descriptive mechanisms exploited by (generative) linguistics; then I will try to show how we can approach an explanation for at least some phenomena, looking at a range of examples from English and elsewhere, and use this extension to substantiate the claim that linguistics is a science. Throughout, I shall concentrate on syntax. Phonology and phonetics, morphology and semantics are rich disciplines in their own right, each with a massive literature, but the essence of the analysis of sentences is their syntactic structure. And life is finite.

III   Describing Knowledge of Language

Sentences have structure of various different kinds. Returning to the example, *My friend likes the penguins*, we need to describe it in different ways at several distinct 'levels of representation': phonological, semantic and syntactic. Thus, it can be pronounced in a variety of ways – with stress on *friends* or on *penguins*, for instance, with concomitant differences of interpretation. Restricting attention to the syntax, it is intuitively clear that *my* and *friend*, and *the* and *penguins*, 'go together' in a way that *friend* and *likes*, and *likes* and *the*, do not. Each of *My friend* and *the penguins* enables us to pick out some individual or individuals in the world, whereas *friend likes* and *likes the* have no such function. This intuition is accounted for in terms of 'constituency', represented by means of a simplified tree diagram of the kind in (22):

22.

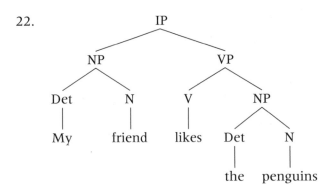

The top of the tree (IP) indicates that the whole sequence *'My friend likes the penguins'* is an 'I(nflection) P(hrase)'(it used to be called 'Sentence', but the terminology has changed to reflect changes in our understanding). The IP 'branches' into an NP and a VP, where 'NP' means 'Noun Phrase' – that is, a sequence consisting of a Noun (N) and something else – and 'VP' stands for 'Verb Phrase' – that is, a sequence consisting of a Verb (V) and something else, here another Noun Phase. The verb is the (present-tense) form *likes,* and the two Noun Phrases each consist of a Noun (here the singular *friend* and the plural *penguins*) preceded by a 'Det(erminer)', respectively *my* and *the.* Each of 'IP', 'NP', 'VP', 'N' etc. are referred to as 'nodes' in the tree; IP, NP and VP etc. are said to 'dominate' everything below them, and to 'immediately dominate' everything immediately below them. So VP dominates all of V, NP, Det, N, *the* and *penguins,* but immediately dominates only V and NP, which are known as 'sisters'. Once one has got used to the jargon. the advantages of such an analysis are many: it simultaneously shows the linear sequence of items – the order they come in – and the relationships among the component parts: so *the* and *penguins* are more closely related, in virtue of being an NP, than are *likes* and *the,* which do not form a 'constituent' of any kind. A constituent is defined as any sequence of items which can be traced exhaustively to a single node in the tree: *likes* and *the* can be traced back to VP (and indeed IP) but these nodes also dominate other material as well (*penguins,* for instance), so *likes the,* like *friend likes,* is not a constituent.

We now have an explicit way of characterizing the example *This school accepts girls and boys under six.* The two interpretations of the object, *girls and boys under six,* can be represented with different constituent structure as in (23):

23a.

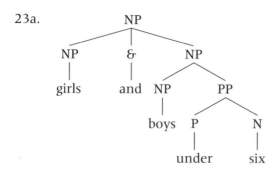

23b.

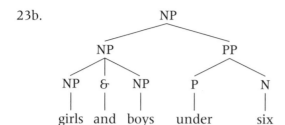

where the tree structure shows the constituents, and indicates that the 'scope' of the Prepositional Phrase (PP) *under six*, where *under* is a Preposition (P), is respectively either just *boys* (23a) or includes *girls and boys* (23b); that is, in each case it pertains to the sister of the PP.

In addition to this syntactic constituent structure, there is morphological structure to deal with: the fact that *penguins* is plural is marked by the addition of the suffix -*s* to the base *penguin*, and the opposite order (with *s*- prefixed to *penguin* to give *spenguin*) is impossible (in English). Investigating the full range of such facts in the world's languages is a matter of intensive research, and addresses the same immediate task of accounting for how it is that native speakers can have the intuitions and make the judgements of well- and ill-formedness that they do.

This last point bears elaborating. One of the surprising facts about our linguistic ability is that it extends to knowing what is impossible as well as what is possible: we have intuitions of ill-formedness or 'negative knowledge'. I have already traded on this fact in assuming that, even though you had probably never heard either example before, you would agree that *Giraffes have necks long* is wrong, whereas *I've just texted an urgent message to Fred* is acceptable. The point can be generalized: the fact that one can recognize mistakes and distinguish them from new but well-formed creations is evidence for the rule-governed nature of the language faculty. In brief, the possibility of making mistakes presupposes the existence of norms or rules. It is also noteworthy that there are 'impossible' mistakes: some logically possible errors just don't happen, even though one might expect them to. Consider an example from language acquisition and the task of the child in working out how questions and statements of the kind in (24) are related:

24a.   The children are playing truant
  b.   Are the children playing truant?

There are all sorts of hypotheses children might entertain: move the auxiliary (*are*), move the third word, permute the first and second constituents, and so on. The kinds of mistake that children do make, however, show that their hypotheses overlap with these in interesting ways. First, they sometimes make mistakes of a kind for which there is no obvious pattern in the input, even though they may be theoretically well motivated: examples like the 'auxiliary copying' in (25):

25a.   Is the steam is hot?
  b.   Are the children are playing truant?

Second, they never try out any hypothesis that would involve them in counting: their attempts always range over modifications of linguistic structure, never of mathematical structure. It seems that all rules in all languages are what is called 'structure-dependent' – they depend on notions like constituent, Noun Phrase, and so on, **not** 'third word'. Moreover, children seem not to need to learn this fact – it is a principle that guides their language acquisition from the start: it is innate. Claims of innateness have been unnecessarily controversial in modern linguistics. No one doubts that humans are innately (genetically) different from cats, chimpanzees and dolphins, and that this difference underlies our ability to acquire language. Equally, no one doubts that humans acquire different languages depending on the environment they are brought up in: if children are brought up in Turkey rather than Greece, they learn Turkish rather than Greek. It is obvious that both nature and nurture have a crucial role to play. Where controversy is justified, and where empirically different claims can be tested, is in the detail of what needs to be ascribed to the child's 'initial state', of what precisely is innate and what has to be acquired on the basis of experience. Explaining structure-dependence is an area where innateness has been repeatedly (and controversially) defended with a form of argument based on the 'poverty of the stimulus' – the idea that we end up knowing things that it is impossible, or at least implausible, to think that we could find in the input. Consider examples more complex than those above, such as (26):

26a.   The children who were naughty are playing truant
  b.   Are the children who were naughty playing truant?

If 'moving the third word' or 'moving the (first) auxiliary' were really linguistically possible ways of characterizing the relation in (24) one would expect to find example mistakes like that in (27):

27a.   Who the children were naughty are playing truant?
  b.   Were the children who naughty are playing truant?

Such mistakes simply do not occur. Of course, it is always (usefully) dangerous to say that something does not happen: it may happen in the next utterance one comes across. But this means that the claim is eminently falsifiable (see below), and can anyway be checked by looking for relevant counter-examples in the literature. A nice case of this kind is provided by Neeleman and Weerman's (1997) account of acquisitional differences between Dutch and English. They predicted that Dutch children should, and English children should not, produce sentences with an adverb intervening between a verb and its object, as in (28):

28.   I will eat quickly the yoghourt

They ransacked the largest international corpus of child data in checking their predictions, and happily found no exceptions.

Formalizing our knowledge of language demands a complex tool-kit, only a tiny fraction of which has been given here, but such formalization is a necessary prerequisite to finding explanations, to assimilating linguistics to the scientific enterprise. Given the tools developed here, we can make general hypotheses about the nature of language and begin to test them on a wider range of data from English and elsewhere.

IV   Explanation in Language

Examples involving structure-dependence enable one to address the demand for explanation in addition to description. Let's pursue the issue by looking at the occurrence of items like *any, ever*, or *anything* in English (so-called 'polarity items'). At a descriptive level it is sufficient simply to contrast possible and impossible sentences of the sort seen in (29), where those in (29a) are fully acceptable but those in (29b) are ungrammatical, or infelicitous, or just wrong:

29a.   John ate something/ some salad
  b.   *John ate anything/ any salad

But *why* is there this contrast? The example in (30) shows that *any(thing)* can occur happily enough in negative statements, but it occurs unhappily in positive statements:

30.   John didn't eat anything/ any salad

Looking at such negative examples, the generalization seems to be that *any(thing)* needs to occur with (be 'licensed by') a negative. But such an account is inadequate in two different ways: first, (31) shows that it is not just negatives that are relevant, because a variety of elements behave in a similar fashion. This class includes questions, conditionals and other items that there is no space to characterize:

31a.   Did John eat anything/ any salad?
  b.   If John ate anything/ any salad, I'd be amazed
  c.   Everyone who has any sense has left already
  d.   John denied having eaten any of the cakes

Second, even if we restrict ourselves to negatives, it still seems that life is more complicated than we might wish – (32a) is unsurprisingly fine but, despite being negative, (32b) is unacceptable and none of (32c) to (32e) is acceptable either:

32a.   Something/ some spider bit him in the leg
  b.   *Anything/ any spider didn't bite him in the leg
  c.   *Anything is annoying me
  d.   *Anything isn't annoying me
  e.   *John denied any of the accusations

That is, our first approximation that *any* needs to be licensed by a negative fails in both directions – some sentences with negatives do not allow *any*; some sentences without a negative do allow *any*. The next obvious assumption might be that *any(thing)* has to be **preceded** by a negative of some kind (*not* or *n't* here),[5] but (33) shows that this hypothesis is inadequate: it works for (33a) and (33b) but not for (33c) or (33d) – where *nothing* is another negative:

33a. The fact that he has come won't change anything
  b. Nothing will change anything
  c. *The fact that he hasn't come will change anything
  d. *That nothing has happened will change anything

The examples in (33) suggest another possibility: perhaps the negative has to be in the same clause as the item (*any*) being licensed? In (33a) the negative and *anything* are in the same clause (compare '*This won't change anything*') whereas in (33c) and (33d) the negative is in a different clause. We are getting closer, but (34) shows that this is still inadequate as an explanation, as here the negative and *anything* are blatantly in different clauses, but the result is well-formed.

34. I don't think he has eaten anything

So the claim that the negative (or other item) must be in the same clause as *any* also fails: some sentences have the negative in a different clause and are nonetheless grammatical; some have the negative in the same clause and are ungrammatical. The correct explanation requires an appeal to the notion of 'c-command', a relation between 'nodes' in a tree. To make this comprehensible and plausible, we need to introduce a little more of the technical machinery of generative grammar.

The representation of sentence structure in terms of trees of the kind shown in (22) can obviously be extended to show the structure of (29a), as shown in (35), where the only novel feature is the uncontroversial claim that *some* is a kind of determiner:

35.

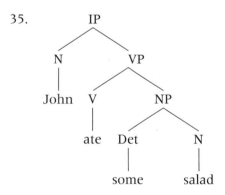

More complex sentences require more complex configurations. Thus, the salient property of an example like (33a) *'The fact that he has come won't change anything'* is that the subject is not just a noun or Noun Phrase, but a Noun Phrase containing another sentence *'he has come'*. To a first approximation it would have the (simplified) form given in (36), and the ungrammatical example in (33c) **The fact that he hasn't come will change anything* would be characterized by the tree given in (37):

36.

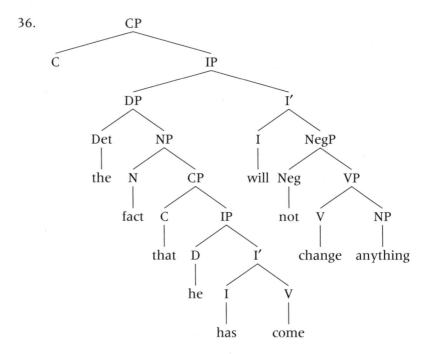

Some of the details of the tree have been included for the sake of those who are familiar with syntax. So the Complementizer Phrase (CP), optionally headed by a complementizer such as *that*, and the I′ (a constituent intermediate in size between a sentence (IP) and an Inflection element like *will*) are there for the cognoscenti. But two things in these trees are important for everyone: first, that they contain a constituent Neg(ation), itself a subpart of a NegP(hrase); and second, that it makes sense to talk of one item being higher in the tree than another. That is, in (36) the 'Neg' is higher in the tree than *anything*, whereas in (37) the 'Neg' is lower in the tree than *anything*.

37.

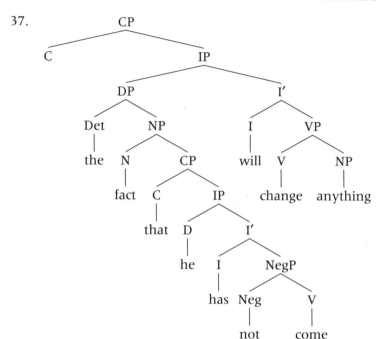

To make this account rigorous we need to define exactly what is meant by 'higher' and 'lower', and that is what is meant by 'c-command': a node A in a tree c-commands another node B if and only if the first branching node dominating A also dominates B. In (36), Neg c-commands *anything* because the first branching node above Neg (i.e. NegP) also dominates the NP *anything*; in (37) Neg does **not** c-command the word *anything* because the first branching node above Neg (again NegP) does **not** dominate *anything*.

It may seem as if we are using a sledge-hammer to crack a nut, but the beauty of the analysis is that c-command is not just an arbitrary condition introduced to account for a narrow range of data in English. Rather it extends in two directions: it is a major and essential ingredient in the explanation first of a range of other phenomena in English, and second of a wide range of phenomena in other languages, indeed in all languages: c-command is universal.

Before illustrating other uses of c-command, note that if it is universal, we would like an explanation for how that is possible. The obvious answer is that it is innate, part of the faculty of language that differentiates humans from other organisms and explains why all kids but no kittens acquire language. If this is correct, certain implications follow immediately: c-command is not a condition that children acquiring their first language need to learn; rather (like structure-dependence) it acts as a constraint that determines the kind of hypotheses they can come up with in mastering their first language.

Let us look at one generalization of the usefulness of c-command in English: its use in 'binding theory', the part of linguistics that deals with the distribution of pronouns and reflexives. It is a commonplace that reflexive pronouns like *myself, yourself, himself,* and so on have to agree (or 'be compatible') with their antecedent – the entity they refer back to; so the examples in (38) are fine, but those in (39) are ungrammatical:

38a.   I admire myself
   b.   The judge admires himself
   c.   The waitress might flatter herself

39a.   *I admire yourself
   b.   *He admires herself
   c.   *The waitress flattered ourselves

There are all sorts of other interesting complications with reflexives: if there are two possible antecedents, the sentence is ambiguous, so in (40) *herself* can refer to either *the nurse* or *the woman*:

40.   The nurse showed the woman some documents about herself

but this is true only if the two potential antecedents are in the same clause as the reflexive: (41) is unambiguous, and *herself* can refer only to *the princess*, because *the queen* is in a different clause:

41.   The queen said the princess had disgraced herself

Neither of these extra considerations accounts for why (42a) is un-ambiguous and (42b) is simply ungrammatical:

42a.   The mother of the princess has disgraced herself
   b.   *The brother of the princess has disgraced herself

The question is why *herself* in (42) can't refer back to *the princess*, but only to the *mother* (in 42a) or, anomalously, the *brother* (in 42b), resulting in the grammaticality judgements indicated. The answer is that the antecedent of the reflexive must not only be compatible and in the same clause as the reflexive, but must also c-command it. The structure of possessive phrases like *the princess's mother* or *the mother of the princess* is a matter of contention, but what is not in dispute is that *princess* is lower in the tree than *mother* or *brother* and hence does not c-command the reflexive: compare the trees in (43) for (38c) and (42):

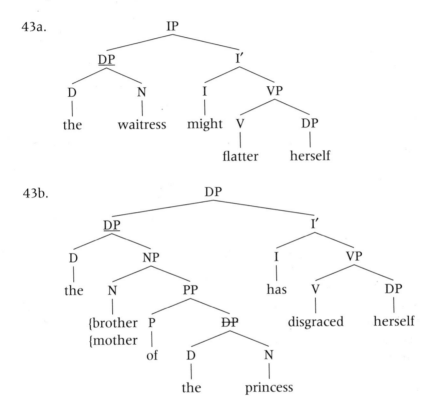

In both trees the underlined DP (*The waitress* in (43a), *The brother/ mother of the princess* in (43b)) c-commands *herself*, but the crossed-out DP *The princess* in (43b) does not c-command *herself* so cannot act as its antecedent.

C-command is pervasive in the syntax of English, not just in accounting for polarity items and reflexives. More strikingly, it is pervasive in the syntax of every other human language.[6] Consider (Cantonese) Chinese. Cantonese has a rich selection of sentence-final particles whose meanings range from conveying a feeling of intimacy to indicating which element in the preceding sequence is the focus. In English we can indicate this focus by means of stress, giving rise to the kind of difference in (44):

44a.   John only **watches** football (he doesn't play it)
  b.   John only watches **football** (not cricket)

It's even possible, with suitable pause and stress, for (45a) and (45b) to have the same interpretation:

45a.   Only **John** watches football (not Bill)
  b.   **John** only, watches football (not Bill)

Just as in English, Cantonese uses stress to identify the intended focus from the set of possible foci, and the operator *zaa3 (only)*[7] then associates with this intended focus, as in (46), which can have the various interpretations shown in (47):

46.   Billy tai zukkau zaa3
      Billy watch football zaa3

47a.   Only **Billy** watches football (not Peter)
  b.   Billy only **watches** football (he doesn't play it)
  c.   Billy only watches **football** (not cricket)

There is good evidence (see Law, 2004) that *zaa3* occurs in the complementizer position of the sentence, and hence in the example in (46) c-commands everything preceding it: see the tree in (48), where C is shown as being sentence-final in Cantonese, not initial as it is in English):[8]

48.

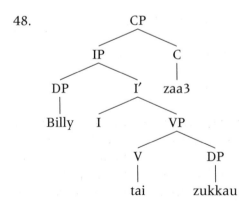

But to talk simply in terms of linear precedence or word order is inadequate. Cantonese also has a process of topicalization whereby a constituent – such as *zukkau* ('football') – can be moved to the front of the sentence, where it is attached even higher in the tree than *zaa3*, and marked with *le1* (the 1 indicates a high level tone). This is shown in (49a), with a range of putative translations in (49b–d). Crucially, as indicated by #, (49d) is **not** a possible interpretation of the Cantonese sentence.

49a.   zukkau-le1, Billy tai t zaa3
  b.   Football, only Billy watches
  c.   Football, Billy only watches
  d.   #Only football does Billy watch

Why this should be so is indicated in the tree in (50), where *zukkau* is not c-commanded by *zaa3* (the 't', for 'trace', in (49a) and (50) indicates where the topicalized constituent *zukkau* moved from):

50.

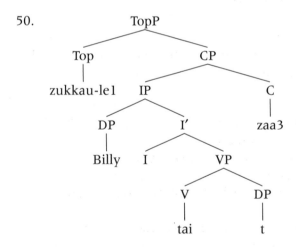

Because *zaa3* does not c-command *zukkau*, the attempted interpretation in (49d) is simply impossible. The examples are extremely simple, indeed extremely over-simplified, but the moral is clear: the same abstract syntactic condition (c-command) operates in Chinese just as it does in English, and every other language.

It is worth emphasizing that successful explanations for one class of data are good to the extent that they generalize to phenomena for which they were not devised. C-command was not invented to account for Chinese, but the fact that it automatically accommodates quite subtle data in that language lends support to any theory which incorporates it. The point can be illustrated more widely. Every time one draws a tree of the kind illustrated above, one makes predictions about the well-formedness of a host of other sentences. For instance, the trees in (36) and (37) claim that *the fact that he has (not) come* is a constituent, but that *the fact* is **not** a constituent, with very specific implications for what can move, what can be coordinated, what can be replaced with a pro-form (see the glossary) such as *it*, and so on. Moreover, it is striking that these trees also exhibit a defining property of human language – its recursive power. That is, the possibility of including one sentence inside another sentence, potentially without limit and in every language in the world, is what gives rise to the infinite expressive power of natural language syntax.

V   Linguistics as a 'Science'

Making testable predictions of this kind is one of the hall-marks of science, and we can now elaborate on the claim that linguistics is 'scientific'. For any discipline to be scientific it must satisfy (at least) the conditions in (51):

51a.   It must seek **explanation**.
  b.   It must pursue **universals**.
  c.   This will necessarily involve **idealization**, which may well give rise to a tension between common sense and science.
  d.   Most crucially, it will make **falsifiable predictions**.

The scientific enterprise is a search for explanatory laws or principles. That is, linguists – like physicists or molecular biologists – seek not only data, but data that can be used as **evidence** for some theoretical claim. Consider again the analysis of reflexives. Early work in linguistics of the sort best exemplified by the work of Bloomfield (1935) provided detailed exemplification of a wide range of reflexive constructions from a variety of languages, but stopped short of trying to explain their distribution. One of the achievements of generative grammar has been precisely to explain – in terms of 'binding theory' – why reflexive pronouns have the distribution they do. To elaborate a little on the discussion given in section IV, the appearance of a reflexive pronoun is determined by principle A of binding theory, which says that a reflexive must be 'bound' in some domain. As we saw, this means that it must have an antecedent which also meets a number of other conditions. Principle A is in contrast with principle B, which determines the distribution of 'ordinary' pronouns. That is, between them the principles account for the range of facts discussed above as well as for the contrast between *John admires him* and *John admires himself*; why one can construe *John* and *him* as referring to the same person in (52b) but not in (52a), even though the latter seems to include the former as a proper sub-part, and a host of other facts:

52a.   John expects to see him
  b.   I wonder who John expects to see him

Evidence for – or against – the claims of binding theory, or any part of the theoretical edifice, can be drawn from a wide variety of domains: the distribution of words in sentences; the acquisition of their first language by children, and of second and subsequent languages by both children and adults; the historical change of language over time; the processing of language – be it production or perception – in normal and abnormal circumstances; the problems that arise in pathology, as a result of language disturbance caused by a stroke or a tumour, and so on. In every case, explanation calls for concentration on those data that can provide evidence: the data themselves are trivial until embedded in a theory that can produce testable hypotheses.

A concomitant of this search for explanation is that the generalizations made must carry over in relevant ways to all languages, not just to English or Latin or Chinese. That is, the quest for laws entails that any science must pursue universals, even if that means narrowing the domain of inquiry. This position has two implications: first, that the same principles that are used in the description of English should apply to Dutch and Hindi and Chinese – so 'all languages' is to be construed literally; but second, that the domain of application of these principles may not be superficially obvious. To take the second observation first, it is well known that if one includes under the heading 'reflexives' everything that includes the morpheme {*self*}, there are problems with so-called 'emphatic' reflexives, as illustrated in (53):

53a.   John himself came
  b.   John came himself

These 'reflexives' have somewhat different properties from 'real' reflexives: for instance, they don't have any thematic role (*came* takes only one argument – you can't 'come somebody else'), but simply emphasize the importance of the one role mentioned. On the other hand they clearly do obey some of the same constraints as ordinary reflexives, as witness the peculiarity of the examples in (54):

54a.   *The boy came herself
  b.   *The boy's mother himself came

This duality of behaviour suggests that it might be necessary – as a temporary measure – to limit the domain of binding theory to arguments taking a thematic role, leaving the emphatic examples to be accommodated later after further research. The situation is parallel to the development of a scientific theory of motion. For Aristotle, all motion fell within the ambit of his theory of movement, even the movement of flowers growing. Galileo was able to provide a unified account of terrestrial and heavenly motion by restricting attention to mechanical motion and excluding biological growth. This should not be viewed as a retreat to a position where whatever you say turns out to be true, simply because you have excluded those areas where what you say is false. Rather it is an attempt to define an area where we can begin to understand the complexity of the real world by focusing on phenomena which are comprehensible.

This narrowing is of two kinds: first, one can simply ignore data which fall outside the generalization one is attempting to explain; second, there is scientific idealization – the pretence that things are simpler than they really are. This is justified because such simplification enables one to approach an understanding of the abstract principles which underlie complex phenomena. Such idealization in linguistics was first made explicit in Chomsky's distinction between competence and performance and his claim that 'linguistic theory is concerned primarily with an ideal speaker-listener, in a completely homogeneous speech-community' (Chomsky, 1965:3). We all know that real speech-communities are not homogeneous, but the force of the idealization is that the heterogeneity that does exist is not a necessary component in an adequate characterization of our knowledge of language or how we come by that knowledge. Consider in this latter respect the simplifying assumption – the striking idealization – that first language acquisition is 'instantaneous'. It is obvious that children take a considerable time to master the intricacies of their first language. Given how complex the knowledge they end up with is, it may still be justifiable to talk of the surprising speed with which they reach this mastery, but it is **not** by any stretch of the imagination 'instantaneous'. So what is the force of the assumption? Consider the acquisition of negation.

Most, perhaps all, children go through a stage in which they produce negative sentences with the negative marker (*no* or *not* in English) in peripheral position in the sentence – that is, first or last – as in (55), heard from two different two-year-olds:

55a.   No computer on
  b.   Computer on no

The context made it clear in each case that the force of the utterance was an order not to turn the computer on. Superficially it looks as if the two children have different grammatical systems (though they were equally proficient at understanding adult instructions, suggesting that their grammar was more sophisticated than might appear). What is relevant here, however, is the fact that – as far as is known – both children will end up with the same grammatical knowledge of English negation. That is, the different stages they go through in their acquisition of the details of the grammar have no effect on the knowledge they end up with – their adult competence. This claim may, of course, be false. It might turn out that adults who uttered (55a) as children have different grammars from those who uttered (55b) as children. It's possible, but there is no evidence to that effect, and the idealization to instantaneity is accordingly justified. If one of the things we wish to explain is how humans can progress from a stage in which they are apparently language-less to a stage of adult knowledge, it is advantageous to be able to abstract away from the different paths they may take in acquiring that knowledge. The idealization also simplifies the account of the initial state of the language faculty: what needs to be attributed to the mental make-up of human infants to explain the fact that they do, while infant chimps do not, acquire language.

Idealization of this kind is in turn likely to involve a tension between common sense and science. The claim of instantaneous language acquisition seems blatantly silly until one considers more carefully what it means. Consider a second example, again from first language acquisition. Children regularly mispronounce the words they are learning, sometimes with surprising results, as in the case of the puzzle puzzle. When he was about two and a half, my son – like many children – used to pronounce *puddle* as 'puggle' ([pʌgəl]). He was perfectly consistent, and used to pronounce words of a comparable kind with the same kind of deformation: so *bottle* became 'bockle', *pedal* became 'peggle', and so on. The obvious explanation for this behaviour was that, for reasons of motor control, he was unable to pronounce *puddle*. But at the same time as he made this mispronunciation, he was also making 'mistakes' with words like *zoo*, pronounced as 'do', *lazy*, pronounced as 'lady', and so on. The result was striking: although he pronounced *puddle* as 'puggle', he consistently pronounced *puzzle* as 'puddle' ([pʌdəl]), so the reason for the former 'mistake' could clearly not be that he was incapable of the appropriate motor control. He could pronounce 'puddle', but only as his version of *puzzle*, not for *puddle*. So the common-sense explanation of the phenomenon was wrong. An obvious alternative explanation was that he couldn't hear the difference, but that hypothesis wasn't very much more plausible, as his pronunciations of the two words were consistently different, indicating that he must be able to perceive the contrast. So the second 'obvious' common-sense explanation was equally problematic. The correct explanation was provided by Marcy Macken (1980), who demonstrated that there was a perceptual problem, but not between *puzzle* and *puddle*, rather between *puddle* and *puggle*. Of course, *puggle* is not a word of English, so I had failed to observe relevant examples. Words like *riddle* and *wriggle* provide a straightforward minimal pair, but they had not been in my son's vocabulary. Fortunately, Macken observed that other examples made the case as well as the (missing) minimal pair did. Words like *pickle* were intermittently pronounced 'pittle' ([pitəl]), suggesting that there was indeed perceptual confusion. The puzzle puzzle could only be solved when the difference between a variety of other examples was simultaneously taken into account.

I have gone on about this example at such length because it illustrates the beauty of being (potentially) wrong. The most crucial part of the scientific enterprise is that it makes testable (or 'refutable' or 'falsifiable') predictions. Because my son regularly distinguished *puddle* and *puzzle*, and similar examples, I had claimed explicitly that he had no perceptual problem. Macken showed that I was wrong and, on the basis of my own data, showed *how* I was wrong, leading to an improvement in our general understanding of language acquisition, and the language faculty more generally. Such falsifiability is pervasive in linguistics as in all the sciences, and suggests that many, perhaps all, our hypotheses and principles will be in need of revision when we get a better understanding of what is going on. It follows that binding theory, which I have appealed to above, is probably wrong, and will need replacing by some more sophisticated theory in due course. Again this is to be welcomed, though we must simultaneously guard against the danger of 'naive falsificationism' (see chapter 8 below). There are always going to be contrary data that one's current theory cannot explain. This is not a reason for simply jettisoning the theory and whatever insights it may provide, but is instead a point of departure for refinement and extension. A clear example is provided by the theory of parametric variation, and the striking revision of his earlier work in Chomsky's current 'Minimalist Program'.

I have suggested that, like all principles of the grammar, binding theory should be universal. But there are problems. Even though (virtually) all languages have reflexives, their distribution is subject to slightly different conditions in different languages. Consider again the contrast between (40), *The nurse showed the woman some documents about herself*, and (41), *The queen said the princess had disgraced herself*, where the former is ambiguous but the latter is unambiguous. The contrast was attributed to the fact that (in English) the antecedent of a reflexive must be in the same clause. So far so good, but if one takes equivalent examples in Chinese it turns out that the equivalent of (40) is unambiguous, and the equivalent of (41) is ambiguous. The theory would appear to have been refuted: a prediction was made, it was tested, and found to be false. But simply giving up the theory would be defeatist, and it would also mean giving up the explanation for the data it does account for.

The solution is interesting: the universality of binding theory (and likewise for other sub-theories of the grammar) is maintained, but some latitude is allowed in the definitions involved – they are 'parametrized', as the jargon has it. In this case, all reflexives have to have an antecedent, but language learners have to choose (on the basis of the data they are exposed to) among several other options: whether they are learning a language in which that antecedent has to appear in the same clause or in some other well-defined domain; whether the antecedent has to be a subject or can bear other grammatical relations, and others. In Chinese, the antecedent of a reflexive must be a subject, so (40) is unambiguous; on the other hand, that antecedent does not have to be in the same clause, so (41) is ambiguous. If you are worried that this is too simple a get-out, an analogy with incest may be helpful: all cultures appear to have an incest taboo forbidding sexual relations between (for instance) fathers and their daughters. The taboo is universal. But how that taboo is instantiated is culture-specific: for example, some groups allow cousins to marry, others do not. The situation with regard to language and language learning is somewhat more complex than the cultural example, because there are many more choices to be made. The acquisitional task is more complex than it would have been if all languages were exactly like English, but it is not as severe as one might fear. The idea is that the full range of parametric choices is available to the child prior to experience – they are in some sense innate – and the child's task reduces to choosing from a set of options it already 'knows'.

VI   Beyond Language: Pragmatics and the Language of Thought

We have looked at a wide range of examples illustrating some of our knowledge of phonology, morphology, semantics and (mainly) syntax, but we also have knowledge that goes beyond words and sentences. Consider (56): as a remark about Fred, (56a) is fine, with stress on *bats* as indicated by the bold print, but as a reply to the question in (56b) it is anomalous:

56a.   Fred has written a book about **bats**
  b.   Who has written a book about bats?

Such discoursal knowledge must be distinguished both from syntactic knowledge of the kind that tells us that (57) is ungrammatical:

57.   Fred has written about **bats** a book

and from real-world knowledge of the kind that prompts our scepticism about (58):

58a.   Bananas have legs
  b.   Your saucer is being aggressive again

Someone who utters (56a) in response to (56b) probably needs remedial English lessons; someone who utters either of the sentences in (58) is either a linguist, or telling a joke, or in need of psychiatric help.

This brings us into the realm of pragmatics, our interpretation of utterances in context, and to the relation of language to thought. The examples in (58) are felt to be odd not because of our linguistic knowledge – you get the same effect whatever language you translate them into – but because we know that the world isn't like that. It is our encyclopedic knowledge that tells us this, not knowledge of English. However, when we interpret someone's utterances in some context, we habitually use both our knowledge of English (or whatever other language we are using) and our encyclopedic knowledge. Suppose you hear (3a) *Tom is a problem*. Your knowledge of English vocabulary and grammar provides you with a meaning for the sentence, but it doesn't tell you enough to act. Is your interlocutor looking for sympathy, asking you to do something about it, hoping for a denial? Any or all of these may be what you decide on a particular occasion, but you carry out this construal on the basis of your knowledge of the speaker, of Tom, of your past exchanges with both of them, and so on indefinitely. The core notion involved is what is 'relevant', an idea that has been made explicit in Relevance Theory, an important extension of linguistics. We are now getting beyond the language faculty and can hand over responsibility to other disciplines; but one final question needs to be addressed: what is language for?

There are two standard answers: for communication and for thought. Both answers are true, but both need a little hedging. First, we can obviously communicate without using language, by means of coughs, sniffs, gestures and so on. But language is far more subtle than any other system known: conveying specific negative or conditional propositions by means of gestures or sniffing is not obviously possible. Innumerable other creatures have complex communication systems, but none of them, as far as we know, has anything with the recursive power of human syntax. (See Sperber and Wilson, 1995; Hauser et al., 2002). Second, the system we use to think with must have a great deal in common with the natural languages we speak, but it is not identical to them. The language of thought can include elements that natural languages cannot – visual images, for instance; and natural languages have properties that would be unnecessary, or even unhelpful, in the language of thought – pronouns, for instance. If I tell you that *she is beautiful*, it's of no use to you storing that in memory as 'she' is beautiful; it has to be stored with a name or some other description replacing *she*. Nonetheless, language has a central role in each of these domains, linking perception and articulation on the one hand to thought processes on the other. This means that the output of our language faculty must be 'legible' to these other systems. Language acts as a code linking representations of sound to representations of meaning. These representations must then be in a form which makes it possible for the sensori-motor apparatus to convert them into pronunciations and percepts, and for the conceptual system to use them for thinking, especially inference.

So, linguistics provides an account of each of syntax, phonology, morphology and semantics, and how they relate to each other; pragmatics then tells us how such purely linguistic representations relate to the language of thought – the medium in which we think and carry out inferencing. This relation underlies our ability to interpret the world and the people in it, but the linguistic component is only the first step on the journey. It is only the first step, but it is a necessary step, because it underpins everything else. We normally take someone who utters a sentence – say, 'torture is immoral' – to *believe* the proposition conveyed by that sentence: that torture is immoral; and we expect to be able to predict (at least some of) their actions on the basis of this. It is language that makes this possible, and it is linguistics that illuminates how it makes this possible. We began with the question 'Why bother with linguistics?' The answer should be becoming clear: it enables us to understand one of the most basic attributes of being human – possession of language.

Acknowledgement

This introductory survey appears here for the first time, though an early version of it is scheduled to appear in the *Encyclopaedia of Language and Linguistics* (Brown, in prep.).

Further reading

Many of the issues touched on here are discussed in more detail in Smith (1989a, 2002, 2004).

The 'generative tradition' has revolved around the work of Noam Chomsky; see McGilvray (1999, 2005), Smith (2004) or Winston (2002) for details.

For sociolinguistics, see, for example, Hudson (1996).

On language and the species, see Anderson (2004), Hauser et al. (2002) and references therein.

On language and literature, especially the nature of literary form, see Fabb (2002). He provides interesting speculations and analyses on a range of issues from generative metrics to the pragmatic notion of interpretive use.

On style, especially the difference between real and fabricated confessions, see Crystal (1988:129–31).

The relation (if any) of language to the external world has been an ongoing preoccupation of Chomsky's; for discussion see Smith (2004).

On notions of correctness, see Fromkin et al. (2003:15f).

On why there might be so many languages, see Baker (2001b).

On the relation between the computational system and the lexicon, see Chomsky (1995a). For a radically different view, see Elman (2004).

On Relevance Theory see Sperber and Wilson (1995); Carston (2002).

On the facts of English see, for instance, Huddleston and Pullum (2004).

For introductory treatments of phonology, see Roca and Johnson (1999); Gussenhoven (2002). For semantics, see Heim and Kratzer (1998); Chierchia and McConnell-Ginet (2000); Fromkin (2000).

For elementary introductions to the technicalities of tree diagrams etc. see Radford (2004a, 2004b) or Adger (2003). For dependency grammar, see, for example, Hudson (1990).

For morphological structure, see, for instance, Fromkin (2000:ch.2).

For 'auxiliary copying' see Radford (2004a:128), (2004b:156).
On linguistics as a science, see Chomsky (1994).
On idealization, see Chomsky (1965:ch.1); Smith (2004:10–14).
For the tension between common sense and science, see Wolpert (1992:ch.1).
For 'puzzles', see Smith (1973), (1989a), (2002:49–52); Macken (1980).
For naive falsificationism, see Lakatos (1970).
Minimalism is encapsulated in Chomsky (1995a); see also Adger (2003); Radford (2004a), (2004b).
On parametric variation, see Baker (2001b).
For binding theory, see Harbert (1995); Reinhart and Reuland (1993).
On incest, see van der Berghe (1983).
For pragmatics, see Carston (2002); Sperber and Wilson (1995).
For the language of thought, see Fodor (1975), and chapter 14 below.
On discourse, see Brown (1995).
For 'legibility', see Chomsky (2000b), (2002a).

Notes

1   Some parrots (e.g. Alex; see Pepperberg, 2002) may seem to belie this claim, but even Alex is not claimed to know English the way humans do. Some aphasia (loss of language as a result of brain damage) may result in performance that deviates wildly from the norm, but some vestiges of the original competence must remain to make even this possible.
2   The OED gives no citation for *richen* in the last hundred years, and no entry for *enthick* at all.
3   *text* as a verb occurs in the *OED* from 1599, but not with the sense now current.
4   Even here, one could argue that the crucial contribution is made by the lexical item *and*.
5   Comparable, but slightly different considerations would obtain for questions and conditionals; I ignore these here.
6   This is as usual a controversial and ultimately empirical claim. For discussion see Baker (2001a).
7   The '3' at the end of *zaa* indicates that it is pronounced with a mid level tone. Chinese is a tone language, that is, one where differences of pitch can distinguish otherwise identical lexical items.
8   The account is simplified for clarity. It is probably the case that there is more than one C position. For details and justification see Law (2004).

Part I

Language in the Limit

1

Savants

A being darkly wise, and rudely great.

Alexander Pope, *Essay on Man*

Derek is blind and so mentally impaired that he cannot accurately distinguish four blocks of wood from five, but he is a superlative jazz pianist. Stephen is autistic and cannot look after himself, but he can draw like an angel, producing work comparable in standard to that of the best professionals. Kate has cerebral palsy and Asperger's syndrome, she does not make eye contact, and she has obsessional fixations, yet she is a gifted poet. Michael has minimal command of language and lives in a sheltered community, but he can reduce six-digit numbers to their prime factors in a few seconds. Christopher cannot devise a non-losing strategy for noughts and crosses (tick-tack-toe), but he can read, write, understand and translate over twenty languages.

All of them are savants, people with an island of startling ability in a sea of disability: people like 'Rainman' made famous by Dustin Hoffman's portrayal of an autistic savant in the film of that name. Studies of savants have burgeoned of late – some of the more dramatic cases make good prime-time television – prompting a number of questions: are these people more than a fascinating peepshow to be exploited by ambitious academics? Do they form a conceptually natural class or are they just lumped together because of their curiosity value? Can such pathological cases really tell us something about the human condition? The danger of exploitation is real and has to be resisted, but the answer to all three questions is a guarded 'yes': we can learn much about the nature of the human mind from these cases.

Savant abilities have elicited a wide range of putative explanations, emphasizing the role of everything from reincarnation to eidetic memory. The former suggestion, ardently believed by some fond parents (see Treffert, 1989:121), should be taken with a pinch of salt: corroborative evidence is very meagre. The latter claim, that savants must be blessed with eidetic memory, either visual or auditory, is initially more plausible, but it seems not to be true: it doesn't account for the facts. Before seeing why, and looking at some experimental studies, it is necessary to raise a separate question: is it the case that, as the result of either genetic lottery or compensatory development arising from perinatal trauma, savants' brains are architecturally unlike those of the rest of us? On this view, savants would be like Martians and, although they are fascinating, would be irrelevant to normal human cognition.

With a population whose abnormality derives from a stroke, or a gunshot wound sustained in adulthood, it is straightforward to argue that their peculiarities arise from knocking out a component of the normal brain they were previously endowed with; hence that it makes sense to use their behaviour as evidence relevant to normal structure and functioning. If an aphasic patient loses functional categories but not lexical categories (see e.g. Froud, 2001), we can safely assume that the two types were separately represented before the stroke. By contrast, if a savant's language seems to display no functional categories, we cannot assume that this provides evidence for the normal population in the same way. With subjects who have developed abnormally from birth, or earlier, one is less obviously justified in using them as providing insight into the rest of us (for a cogent elaboration of this position, see Karmiloff-Smith, 1998). This 'Martian hypothesis' is less plausible to the extent that the dissociations and peculiarities one sees in the savant population mirror those in the aphasic population, but evaluating the evidence is always going to be harder in the developmental domain. The shared absence of 'functional categories', for instance, is suggestive but hardly decisive. *Caveat lector*.

So we need evidence. The best is summarized by Ati Hermelin (2001), who has recently devoted a fascinating book to savants, documenting work carried out by the late Neil O'Connor and herself over the previous forty years. It is an invigorating mixture of intellectual austerity and personal passion, and it reveals that savant abilities are not only rule-governed, but explicable in terms of the same theories that are used to account for the activities of less remarkable members of society. Let's look at some examples.

Calendrical calculators can tell you in a few seconds the day of the week for any date they are presented with. If their ability was restricted to the past, it would be plausible to suggest that it was done by superlative, perhaps eidetic, memory; but the fact that for many savants the ability generalizes to the future makes reliance just on memory implausible. More interestingly, it appears that they unconsciously exploit mathematical regularities in the calendar. For instance, the days of the week fall on the same day in March and November: if 1 March is a Wednesday then so is 1 November. Better yet, the days of the week recur in a 28-year cycle: if 13 July 2001 is a Friday, then you can be sure that 13 July 1973 was also a Friday. Fortunately, calendrical calculators are human and so not infallible: they make mistakes, and these mistakes increase the further one moves from the present, either into the past or into the future. They are more accurate identifying days for dates ten years in the future than for days twenty years in the future. But there are systematic improvements in performance when one elicits dates 28 or 56 years removed from the present. The obvious explanation is that they 'know' the regularity of the 28-year cycle.

The same kind of rule-governed ability is characteristic of musical savants. There are many stories of severely retarded, often speech-less, people being able to play complex pieces of music after hearing them just once or twice. This talent is not that of a tape-recorder, but is crucially dependent on the structure of the music being played. In collaboration with John Sloboda (see Sloboda et al., 1985), Hermelin and O'Connor tested one autistic musical prodigy and compared him with a professional musician. The results were striking: the savant was dramatically better than the professional at reproducing a previously unheard piece of tonal music by Grieg (*Melodie*, Op. 47 No. 3), but markedly worse than the professional at playing back a piece of atonal music by Bartok (the *Whole tone scale* from Book 5 of *Mikrokosmos*). The implication is that the savant's ability is not just the result of a wonderful memory and remarkable manual dexterity, but is structure-dependent, a conclusion borne out by his ability to engage in appropriate improvisation in the tonal domain.

Such structure-dependence should remind you of linguistic abilities. Another savant who features elsewhere in both this book (see chapters 3 and 7 below) and its predecessor (Smith, 2002) is Christopher, the polyglot who can perform in any of twenty or more languages (see also Smith and Tsimpli, 1995, 1996; Morgan et al., 2002). He flourishes on a diet of complex morphology and novel lexical input but, like normal controls, failed utterly when we tested him on 'impossible' constructions whose major characteristic was that they were structure-*in*dependent, requiring the speaker to count the number of words before the insertion of an emphatic suffix. The implication is that savants and normals alike manifest behaviour which succumbs to the same kind of theoretical description and explanation.

Even the apparently random feats of memory performed by some autistic savants – like remembering the routes and numbers of every bus in south London – seem to be constrained by the structure of memory, so that the material of special interest to the savant is 'stored in memory in a categorized form' (O'Connor and Hermelin, 1989:97). They ingeniously demonstrated this with tests in which they paired the numbers of buses using the same home garage (47 and 261 both start from Bromley, for instance) or the number of a bus and the name of its home garage (47 and Bromley); and contrasted these with pairs consisting of two fruits (orange and apple), a fruit and a vegetable, a fruit and a number, a number and a vegetable (133 and radish), and so on. After suitable training, the subjects were tested on their ability to recall the various pairs. The results were striking: the subjects reacted differently to the different conditions, doing significantly better in their obsessional domain than in other arbitrary conditions, and markedly better than normal controls. They were not simply relying on rote memory.

What can we learn from cases like these? The most obvious implication is that they provide evidence for some version of the modularity hypothesis. If striking talent can coexist with severe intellectual impairment, then this suggests rather strongly that such talent, whatever form it takes, need not be dependent on a high level of intelligence. If Fodor (1983) is right about the division of human cognition into a central system and a set of modular input systems, then it follows that each component can be impaired selectively, with one possibility being a central deficit in 'intelligence'. This might seem to suggest that there is a module for each savant obsession. Many savants do indeed have talents in domains that are apparently subserved by modular architecture: mathematics, music and language, for instance. But no one wants to suggest that we have a module dedicated to the calendar, or bus timetables, or cartoon characters. The dissociation between intelligence and other abilities is correct, and is presumably underpinned by common neural architecture, but the range of savant obsessions goes beyond that architecture.

Most savants are autistic, and part of the 'cognitive style' of such people is that they focus on the separate elements of each domain, and typically fail to integrate them into a coherent whole (Happé, 1999; Hermelin, 2001). Does this characteristic have as some compensation that it licenses the abilities I have been documenting? The answer is not clear, but it is suggestive that even autistic children without obvious talents do better in some (musical) tests than matched control subjects. Hermelin (2001:170f) reports that 'musically naïve autistic children show superior pitch identification ability', and when asked to disassemble tonic triads, where each note of a chord was associated with an animal, and the task was to identify the missing animal, 'children with autism gave more correct responses than the control children whose performance was at chance'.

Most savants are autistic, but not all savants are. If the cognitive style of focusing on detail rather than the whole gestalt is at the root of their abilities, then it must either be the case that a comparable cognitive style is also characteristic of non-autistic savants, suggesting the need for an account which abstracts away from autism; or it suggests that savants are not a natural class after all. Deciding between these, and other, alternatives is a desirable academic ambition, which can be pursued while we marvel at the abilities on display.

Acknowledgement

A version of this chapter appeared in 2001 in *Glot International* 5:243–5.

Further reading

On double dissociation in aphasia and á careful discussion of cognitivist versus associationist explanations for such dissociations, see Caramazza and Shapiro (2004).

For recent work on the genetics of autism with special reference to the savant syndrome, see Nurmi et al. (2003).

For parallels between music and language, see Patel (2003).

2

Singing by the Dead

the communication
Of the dead is tongued with fire beyond the language of the living.
            T. S. Eliot, 'Little Gidding' (*Four Quartets*)

Death confers a certain cachet. Once an artist is dead, his or her creations form a closed set that can never be augmented. Pride of ownership and security of scholarly opinion can remain unchallenged by inconvenient additions that might force a change of mind. The same attitude often seems to attach to languages. Once they are safely dead and no longer subject to irritating change, they can be admired and codified, and put on display for the delectation of the philologist and the consternation of the student. George Steiner (1998:57) sums up the feeling admirably with the remark that: 'a number of dead languages are among the obvious splendours of human intelligence'. If this were interpreted as a remark about the literature written in those languages, few would disagree: Homer and Virgil have deservedly survived for millennia, and contemporary rivals in literary stature do not spring readily to mind. In fact, Steiner appears to have meant what he said literally; the quotation continues: 'Many a linguistic mastodon is a more finely articulated, more "advanced" piece of life than its descendants.'

This yearning for past beauty is certainly in tune with the thinking of the linguistic blimps and mavens who take it on themselves to act as guardians of the purity of English, or French or Icelandic: the golden age is never the present. But linguists presumably have no such preconceptions; rather we tend to believe, quite often without marshalling much evidence, that every language is as good as any other. The standard shibboleth is that 'whatever you can say in your language I can say in mine – and vice versa'. So presumably the linguistic descendants of Homer and Virgil – speakers of modern Greek and of the Romance languages – have command of languages every bit as 'finely articulated' as their ancestors. All languages are equal, even if some are more equal than others in virtue of having a rich written literature, or of being spoken by people who are dominant for reasons of military, political or economic domination. Native speakers of English have a variety of advantages that are denied native speakers of Welsh or Warlpiri (such as benefiting automatically from the TEFL and TESL industry), but there is no evidence that such advantages are a result of the linguistic properties of English.

This predilection for the dead is pervasive. Many have spoken forcefully of the desirability of the hegemony of English, even to the extent of arguing that we need more dead languages. C. K. Ogden, who invented 'Basic English', and was working on the assumption that there were about 1,500 'chief languages', suggested that: 'the chief need of our time is 1,480 more dead languages' (1940:96). So if language death brings, on the one hand, prestige and, on the other, an improvement in world communication, should we not welcome it, or at least be neutral towards it? Or should we worry and, if possible, try to do something to stop the extinction of languages just as we try to stop the extinction of cuddly animals?

In an eloquent recent book, David Crystal (2000) lists a number of reasons why we should care: because we need diversity, because languages express our identity, because they are repositories of history, because they contribute to the sum of human knowledge, and because they are interesting in themselves. Are these good reasons?

To start with the last, no linguist could disagree that all languages are interesting in themselves: after all, that's why we devote our lives to them. But it's not so obvious that we need six thousand to work on rather than the six hundred that Crystal says are not in any danger of extinction. He elaborates the argument by pointing out that certain exotic languages (those typically most endangered) have properties not found in those closer to home: clicks, unusual number systems, complex patterns of the morphologization of evidentiality, and so on. If such languages had died before we could codify them, these properties might have been irretrievably lost, to the obvious impoverishment of our subject. A case in point is provided by my own favourite language (Nupe), which I've worked on intermittently since I was a student (see e.g. Smith, 1967), and which is different from most of the languages of the world in virtue of its word order. In most languages, the object either *follows* the verb or it *precedes* the verb. In Nupe the object comes in the middle of the verb. If Nupe were to become extinct (fortunately, it still has about a million speakers), this striking and unusual property might vanish from our ken for ever. But actually Nupe is not as bizarre as this description might indicate, and deeper analysis shows that the 'peculiarity' falls out quite naturally from elementary assumptions about V to I movement. The point is important: what linguistics needs most is depth of analysis, rather than superficial descriptions of more and more data. Unless some benign dictator insists that all future academic work is done on linguistics, six hundred languages is probably a large enough sample to keep the world's linguists busy. So the first argument is inconclusive.

That languages express identity is important and undeniable. Your first language is part of you for ever, just as your parents and siblings and children are yours for ever. No one who has read accounts such as John Milloy's (1999) heart-rending description of the systematic 'language abuse' of Canadian aboriginals could doubt that the language death he describes is pernicious, destructive and should be opposed by every means possible. But he is really describing language *murder*, not just death. Everyone dies, which is sad but natural. Languages die too, and that is also sad but natural. But murder is unspeakable and not natural. The murder of your language can be as demoralizing as the murder of a member of your family, and should be greeted with the same abhorrence.

The same arrogance and greed that can lead to the extermination of languages can lead to the extermination of the cultures that they help preserve, and the disappearance of the history that their texts, written and oral, record. At a time when authorities are trying to manipulate the documentary record in their own interests, revisionist history is essential, and the death of a language closes off a major source of the information prerequisite to such revision. The arguments that Crystal presents to show that we should care about language death seem to me to be overwhelming and unanswerable when applied to language murder. It is not so clear, however, that they apply to natural death of the sort illustrated by the demise of Old English, for instance. Even though it has left descendants (us) and the compensation of a literary heritage, Anglo-Saxon, like Latin and classical Greek, is dead. It is not obvious to me that this is something that either does or should evoke sadness or grief.

What about Crystal's final point – our putative 'need for diversity'? This seems to me to be largely similar to the argument from inherent interest. Quantifying the amount of diversity that is necessary or desirable for 'ecological' reasons is not easy, and I am anyway not convinced that the arguments are any more sound in this domain than in that of wildlife conservation. If it is really true that 'the extinction of any animal species diminishes our world' (Crystal, 2000:36, citing Krauss, 1992) then medical research which seeks to eliminate bilharzia, or malaria, or dengue fever by killing snails or mosquitoes is immoral and should be stopped. Kaplan (2004) makes a related point in his article 'Save the rhino maggot!' (as well as the rhino), arguing that not only is the maggot just as unique as the rhino, but it is probably necessary to the survival of the rhino. Despite such arguments, I find the implicit conclusion that we should save mosquitoes unacceptable, and the ecological parallel unpersuasive. Nonetheless, there is one domain where I think the argument can be made somewhat stronger.

Surprisingly, there is no mention in Crystal's book, or in much of the mainstream 'language death' literature, of sign languages; yet they are endangered just as much as are spoken languages, and they have been historically discriminated against in much the same way as the aboriginal languages have. An interesting example of the disappearance of a signed language is provided by Nora Groce's inspiring (1985) book on the language of the deaf (and hearing) community on Martha's Vineyard. As a result of the immigration from Kent in the seventeenth century of families including a number of deaf people, there developed on Martha's Vineyard a community where *everyone* was bilingual in sign language and English. Indeed, 'for those who lived up-Island, a knowledge of [sign] language was a necessity' (1985:55), and code switching, for example, was a normal, everyday occurrence. Moreover, the advantage of having languages in two modalities was widely and systematically exploited: whether by fishermen communicating from ship to shore, or by people visiting relatives in hospital when these were deemed too ill to 'speak'.

What is most remarkable about Groce's account is the picture it paints of a community where deafness was in no way stigmatized, caused no disadvantage or social exclusion, and was not even noticed as remarkable until outsiders commented upon it. 'You know, we didn't think anything special about them [the deaf]. They were just like anyone else. When you think about it, the Island was an awfully nice place to live' (1985:110). When one compares this scenario with the catalogue of discrimination inflicted upon the deaf elsewhere in the States and in Europe, where signing has often been systematically prohibited, often under threat of inhuman punishment, it reveals a positively Utopian situation. Indeed, it was only in 2003 that the UK government belatedly recognized British Sign Language (BSL) as a language. Previously, the absence of a 'written form' had led to the conclusion that it wasn't a proper language at all.

The sign language of Martha's Vineyard predated and was distinct from the early stages of American Sign Language (ASL), first documented from around 1817. There does appear to have been some mutual influence but, whereas ASL is flourishing, the island sign language is extinct. The reason is that since the mid-twentieth century the population has no longer included the substantial proportion of deaf people that it once did. From one perspective, this is perhaps a kind of progress: if deafness is viewed as a disability, the decrease in the numbers of the deaf is presumably to be welcomed. But from another perspective, it is a tragedy. Not only have we lost a natural language which could have cast interesting light on the development of signed languages around the world, but we have also lost one of the most positive achievements of any human society: the living together in bilingual harmony of deaf and hearing people, where neither was viewed as better than – or even significantly different from – the other. This is a far cry from the current situation where the uncomprehending attitude of the majority hearing community has led to an intermittently acrimonious debate about whether deafness is something in need of 'curing' at all (see Hagan, 2004).

If one generalizes the arguments about language death to include signed languages, I think that they become more persuasive, so I conclude with the belated realization that my original title may have been not only somewhat baffling, but also wrong – a simple typographical error. It should have been: 'Signing by the Deaf'.

Acknowledgements

A version of this chapter first appeared in 2001 in *Glot International* 5:98–100.

I am grateful to Bencie Woll both for suggesting the title to me and for drawing Groce's book to my attention.

Further reading

The literature on language death is increasing rapidly year by year: see Janse and Tol (2003) for a typical example, or just enter 'language death' on Google.

The British government's previous attitude to sign language is encapsulated in the following extract from a letter from Sir John Patten, secretary of state for education, in 1993: 'I believe that a language needs to have a cultural heritage and generally a written form permitting access to a body of expression and ideas, literature and common values which, when taken together, are characteristic of it. I could not agree that British Sign Language is comparable to English, or French, or any other language in regular use.'

This is one linguistic battle that has been won.

3

Maganar Hannu

But thou didst understand me by my signs
And didst in signs again parley with sin.

William Shakespeare, *King John*

The chances that you know what the title of this chapter means are pretty remote, so let me tell you. It is in the Hausa language spoken widely in West Africa, especially northern Nigeria, and translates into English as 'Language of the Hands'. The reason for its appearance here is that I have recently been reading a pioneering book on Hausa Sign Language. This might seem to be the most esoteric piece of academic research possible, but its status is no different in principle from that of a grammar of Dutch or an analysis of Scottish English, and can cast just as bright light on the nature of the human language faculty as these can.

As we saw in chapter 2, it has long been widely accepted among linguists that all languages are equal; even if a specialist vocabulary makes it easier for the English speaker to discuss the complexities of genetics and for the Masai to discuss the intricacies of the age-grade system. It is a more recent discovery, dating from the pioneering work of Stokoe (1960) on American Sign Language (ASL), that the sign languages of the deaf have the same expressive power as spoken languages. When I was speaking at an international conference in Boston, the simultaneous interpreter had no more difficulty in translating my lecture into ASL than her colleague did in rendering it into Spanish. Moreover, it is emphatically **not** the case that this expressive power is parasitic on the ambient spoken language. ASL is unrelated to American English, just as BSL

(British Sign Language) is unrelated to British English; and ASL is more closely related to French Sign Language than either is to BSL.

There has been an explosion of research activity into sign languages over the last twenty years, but African sign languages have previously been neglected. Schmaling's (2000) monograph goes a long way to redressing that neglect. Her primary focus is on Hausa Sign Language (HSL): the signed language used by the deaf community in Kano and elsewhere in the country; but she sets this work in the wider context of Hausa studies, including the educational and social context in which deaf people find themselves in Hausa society (and in Nigeria and West Africa, more generally), and adding some discussion of the full range of communicative resources at the disposal of the deaf and hard of hearing.

The core of the book is a grammar of HSL. It begins with a clear and comprehensive account of the four parameters of hand-shape, orientation, location and movement, which form the phonological and morphological basis for HSL as for any sign language. Just as the phonology of spoken languages exploits contrasts in place and manner of articulation, the 'phonology' of signed languages exploits contrasts in the configuration of the hands, their position in the sign-space in front of the body, and the direction of movement of the hands. To these she adds some details of the non-manual components of sign: most notably facial action (furrowed brows, for instance), which can carry both lexical and grammatical information. It is not widely known outside the sign language community that such facial action is a central and crucial component of all signed languages. The treatment is meticulous, extremely detailed, and makes it clear that HSL deserves the title 'language'. Strikingly, the description she provides could equally have been about any other language – signed or spoken – anywhere in the world: the theoretical underpinning of the work appeals to the same constructs and uses the same literature as any other sophisticated contemporary grammar: feature geometry in phonology, affixation and incorporation in morphology, classifiers in syntax.

Schmaling also addresses the vexed question in sign studies of the arbitrariness of signs, discussing the greater role of iconicity in all signed languages – hence in HSL – than in spoken languages. Opponents of sign languages (and there are sadly still many) have used the prevalence of iconic signs, exemplified cross-linguistically by the signs for SEE and TREE,[1] to diminish the value of sign languages, claiming that they are merely gestural. As a result, many sign language researchers have studiously downplayed the role of iconicity in order to prove that their objects of study are 'real' languages. Happily, that battle has been won – at least in so far as the linguistic community is concerned – and Schmaling is therefore able to present the facts impartially. Once one realizes that HSL, again like all languages, has no difficulty representing notions like TRUTH or EMBARRASSMENT, or differentiating future negation from past negation, it is clear that it couldn't possibly be solely iconic, even if up to a third of signs have some iconic value.

One can go further. The iconicity of signed languages is salient to those who know only spoken languages, and may be helpful to learners who are confronted with mastering a signed language for the first time in adulthood. But it is less helpful, perhaps no help at all, to children acquiring sign as a first language. Consider a simple example from BSL: the word for 'milk' is imitative of the action of milking a cow,[2] but this is presumably not common knowledge among the deaf urban two-year-olds who are busy acquiring BSL from their parents and peers. If suitably exposed to cows (or sheep or buffalo, of course) the sign may become iconic for them, but it is clearly not iconic during the learning process. A parallel example in spoken language is the ability of people to learn the onomatopoeic *cuckoo* even though they have never heard the bird.

Even for (some) second language learners, iconicity may not always be as helpful as one might expect. In an ongoing project (see Morgan et al., in prep., and chapter 1 above) we have been investigating the remarkable abilities of a polyglot savant (see Smith and Tsimpli, 1995; Morgan et al., 2002). Christopher lives in sheltered accommodation because he cannot look after himself; he is somewhat autistic, severely apraxic, and finds noughts and crosses (tick-tack-toe) intellectually challenging; yet he can read, write, speak, understand and translate over twenty languages. In an attempt to tease out the various strands of his talents and disabilities, we taught BSL to him and a comparator group of forty talented second language learners, with the aim (among many) of discovering whether his remarkable linguistic ability would generalize to a signed language, or whether his apraxia and autism would inhibit his talent. To cut a long story short, he treated BSL like any other language, but he showed interesting behaviour when it came to iconicity. When members of the control group were subjected to a test in which they were asked to identify previously unknown **iconic** signs, they scored well – better than with non-iconic signs – showing the facilitatory effect of iconicity. Christopher, on the other hand, scored at chance and seemed in general to be impervious to iconic clues. This is perhaps a reflection of his impaired central abilities, and may suggest that he is functioning more like a first language learner in this area than a typical second language learner. Be that as it may, two points emerge clearly. First, it is evident that iconicity is far from exhausting the resources of any sign language; second, the modularity hypothesis discussed earlier (chapter 1 above; see also chapters 9 and 14 below) predicts precisely the kind of dissociation between central and linguistic abilities that seem to be merged in iconicity.

The study of Hausa Sign Language may appear to be a rather esoteric enterprise, but as well as filling a gap in our knowledge, it confirms again that all languages are cut from the same cloth, and so meshes beautifully with research across the whole field.

Acknowledgement

This chapter originated in 2002 as a review of Constanze Schmaling's (2000) *Maganar Hannu: Language of the Hands. A Descriptive Analysis of Hausa Sign Language. International Studies on Sign Language and Communication of the Deaf. Vol. 35.* Hamburg, Signum Verlag. The review appeared in *Africa: Journal of the International Africa Institute* 72:177–8.

Further reading

Interesting parallels with other sign languages can be inferred from looking at Neidle et al. (2000). The discussion of iconicity raises the important issue of the Whorf hypothesis (see chapter. 4 below; and for recent discussion see Majid et al., 2004).

Notes

1   For *see* in BSL 'the index finger taps the cheek below the eye'; for *tree* 'the left arm is positioned across the body; the right elbow is held on the back of the left hand' (imitating a tree standing) (see Brien,

1992). For the Hausa sign language equivalents, see Schmaling (2000:205), where they are described as '(almost) identical or very similar in many sign languages'.

2 The sign is described in the standard BSL dictionary in the following terms: 'The hands are held side by side in front of the body' and 'the hands make alternate short up and down movements' (Brien, 1992:179).

4

Sneering at the Arts

If authors sneer, it is the critic's business to sneer at them for sneering.
William Makepeace Thackeray, *The Newcomes*

It has become fashionable to sneer at the arts and humanities. It is perhaps not surprising when a distinguished scientist like my colleague Lewis Wolpert (professor of biology as applied to medicine at UCL) says that he 'does not take the arts intellectually seriously' (Wolpert, 2002); it is somewhat more worrying when the recipient of the Nobel prize for literature, V. S. Naipaul, suggests that universities should teach only maths and the sciences. He is quoted (Robinson, 2002) as saying that 'Scientists matter. Not the arts courses . . . I would like to see all those arts courses closed down . . . I think universities should be for science and mathematics.'

Linguists, of course, like to think of linguistics as a science (see the introduction above), but it's not clear that we and our departments would survive if such views were implemented. But whose side should we be on? It is true that some of our colleagues in arts departments provide plenty of justification for such sneering. The obvious example of justified contempt is highlighted by Alan Sokal's (1996a) devastating parody of postmodernism in his 'Transgressing the boundaries: toward a transformative hermeneutics of quantum gravity'. Postmodernism – to the extent that it is a coherently definable entity – emphasizes the subjective at the expense of objectivity, and denies the validity of universals, of truth and of rationality. This article, by a distinguished physicist, purported to find parallels between quantum field theory and Lacanian psychoanalysis, between fuzzy logic and left-wing political views, between the axiom of equality in set theory and equality in politics. It was written as a deliberately incoherent hoax, yet appeared in a special number of the journal *Social Text* devoted to the 'Science Wars'. The editors were apparently so pleased with the putative confirmation of their views that no thought of critical evaluation entered their heads. The author then revealed (Sokal, 1996b) that it was a hoax, demolishing the intellectual pretensions of the journal – and the movement – in the process.

In his reflections on the affair, Boghossian (1996) attacks post-modernism for (among other things) its relativistic view of truth: the claim that there is no such thing as scientific objectivity and that truth is a social construct. A linguist might be inclined to generalize the attack to cover its relativistic implications for language. Although there has been a certain renaissance in linguistic relativism of late, some of it perceptive and sophisticated (e.g. many of the papers in Bowerman and Levinson, 2001), the major emphasis in current linguistics is still largely on universals. This would presumably still be anathema to the relativists, and I fear anyway that epithets like 'perceptive' do not really pertain to postmodernism, still less to its most opaque sub-domain – deconstruction.

Consider the view put forward (surprisingly in the pages of *New Scientist*) by Marks (2002), suggesting that a closer, 'deconstructionist', analysis of the language of safety manuals for nuclear power stations might obviate nuclear accidents. This is eerily reminiscent of Benjamin Lee Whorf's (1941:75) claims about how the designation 'empty', when applied to discharged petrol cans, led people to assume that they were really 'empty', and didn't contain explosive vapour, with the result that accidents kept happening. Then as now, what is really needed is explicit training in chemistry, not English lessons in the use of 'empty'. I imagine that any deconstructionist worth his or her salt could do the latter job, but I suspect that the number of such scholars with the right background in nuclear engineering to do the former is not very high.

This is all good healthy fun, where sneering is probably in order, but it is important to separate the pretentious chaff from some rather good wheat: not all arts subjects are so benighted, and I believe that providing insight in a complex domain is sufficient defence for any discipline to be studied in universities. Let me give a couple of examples from the study of English literature. Joseph Brodsky (another Nobel laureate), in an essay (1987) which was originally part of a lecture course given at Columbia University, discusses W. H. Auden and his poem 'September 1, 1939'. Brodsky provides some unremarkable, but useful, factual explanations – the poem starts with a reference to 'Fifty-second street', which everyone can easily identify as picking out Manhattan, but not necessarily that at the time this was 'the jazz strip of the universe' (p. 308) and that there were echoes of jazz syncopation in the metrical structure of the poem, which I at least would otherwise not have realized. Apart from this useful but not particularly profound background information, two things from his exegesis stick in my mind. First, I had read the poem, but had not appreciated many of the allusions he explained, or shared the interpretation that he suggested: for instance, his observation that the work is 'first and foremost a poem about shame' (1987:338). Second, Brodsky's own remarks were full of surprising aphoristic insights: his description of Auden as 'a despairing moralist whose only means of self-control is the iambic trimeter' (p. 325) captures the man beautifully; and his observation that 'uncertainty . . . is the mother of beauty' (p. 339), or his reference to 'the encroachment of American diction' (p. 307) as a stylistic device in the poem, strike me as unusually perceptive. Any sneering here should be directed only at the ignorant reader who needs such help (me, for example).

A second source of great insight (again, for me at least) is Frank Kermode's (2000) book *Shakespeare's Language*. Most of us (well, most of my antique generation) were brought up on Shakespeare, so the need for explanations in this domain might seem superfluous. But, reading Kermode, I was repeatedly struck by what he said, and was not only reminded how much I enjoyed and admired Shakespeare, but was also made to appreciate why I did. Let me illustrate. If any play has suffered from over-exposure it is *Hamlet*, and I have read it, seen it, heard it, and even studied it. But Kermode still gave me fresh insight. There were technical details of the sort that any decent critic provides – pointing out Shakespeare's pervasive use of hendiadys, and how that usage varies from scene to scene (and from play to play). Hendiadys is the rhetorical figure in which two nouns are conjoined to convey what one might have expected to be done by other means: 'rank and station', 'the perfume and suppliance of a minute'. Kermode felicitously calls it 'a way of making a single idea strange by splitting an expression in two' (2000:15). But he also made deeper observations, highlighting its intermittently increased use to slow down the action of the plot; pointing out that this trope is only one aspect of a 'doubling' that imbues the whole play – the play within a play, the status of Laertes as Hamlet's double, and more. Maybe I should have realized all this, but being shown how the Master uses language was illuminating.

Comparable observations apply to *Macbeth*. Concentration on time is central to this play, but I had never got beyond admiring the 'Tomorrow and tomorrow and tomorrow' soliloquy. I had certainly never noticed how the idiosyncratic rhythm of the metrical structure of the play reinforces the effect of the lexical choices, as in Banquo's words to the witches:

> If you can look into the seeds of time,
> And say which grain will grow, and which will not,
> Speak then to me, who neither beg nor fear
> Your favours nor your hate.

The whole of this scene highlights systematic alternations: between past and future, fair and foul, positive and negative, Macbeth and Banquo. I found myself reading it differently after thinking about Kermode's analysis. Discussing the same section, he also suggests that we are meant to apprehend the 'imperfect speakers' (the witches), their characters and their actions, 'imperfectly'. This licence not to understand came as something of a revelation to me, and also prompted further musing. 'Imperfect' not only brings with it overtones of incomprehension arising from the difficulty of some of the play's language but, to a linguist, also suggests aspectual incompleteness, opening up whole new areas for speculation.

Such reinterpretations may not be justifiable, but the deliberate use of obfuscatory complexity is evident in much of Shakespeare's later work, most strikingly in *Coriolanus*. I first saw this play without ever having read it, but the eponymous hero was played by Sir Laurence Olivier, and the effect was overwhelming. I was even pleased with myself for (I thought) appreciating most of its language. I hadn't realized how little I had really followed; still less that in some instances, I hadn't been intended to follow it. Kermode draws a striking contrast between the transparency of Marcus's address to his mutilated niece Lavinia in *Titus Andronicus* and the impenetrability of much of Aufidius's meditation on his ally and former enemy, Coriolanus. I had never been able to suspend my disbelief in the former speech, but after Kermode's historical contextualization, I at least understood what Shakespeare was doing. But his discussion of the latter speech was revelatory: it is 'ominously obscure' (2000:15) and 'deliberately made to involve us in daunting ambiguities' (p. 254). Consider the bewildering lines:

> . . . whether defect of judgment,
> To fail in the disposing of those chances
> Which he was lord of; or whether nature,
> Not to be other than one thing, not moving
> From the casque to the cushion, but commanding peace
> Even with the same austerity and garb
> As he controll'd the war; but one of these
> (As he hath spices of them all, not all,
> For I dare so far free him) made him fear'd,
> So hated, and so banish'd; but he has a merit
> To choke it in the utt'rance.

in which Aufidius is 'worrying over a perhaps insoluble problem' (2000:16) and where representing 'the movement of thought' takes precedence over clarity. I hadn't realized how Shakespeare, through Aufidius, was manipulating the onlookers (including me) by 'not painting a picture for the audience but trying to make clearer to himself just how mixed his feelings are' (2000:15). As linguists, we trade in daunting ambiguities, and I should perhaps have been more aware of what Shakespeare was doing. I wasn't; but now I am, and I am grateful to Kermode.

If you're going to sneer – be selective.

Acknowledgement

This chapter first appeared in 2003 in *Glot International* 7:73–5.

Further reading

For recent discussion of the Whorf hypothesis, see Majid et al. (2004); Gentner and Goldin-Meadow (2003).

5

Babes and Sucklings

Out of the mouth of babes and sucklings hast thou ordained strength.
Psalms 8.2

These sucklings are pretty impressive.

They may look useless and make a lot of noise, but in the first few months of life they display some dazzling talents. They can not only recognize Mum and an assortment of other people's faces and voices, they can also correlate these faces and voices according to the age of their owners (Bakrick et al., 1998); they can recognize by sight forms that they have coded by touch in the dark; they can identify the numerosity of items and events, responding differentially to cards with different numbers of spots on; and they have expectations of number, showing surprise when two dolls appear where one or three are predicted (Butterworth, 1999; Dehaene, 1997; Wynn, 1998). They can mentally represent states of affairs that they can no longer perceive, showing that they understand the 'continuity' and 'solidity' of a variety of objects – though the poor things have serious problems with gravity and inertia until they are about a year old (Spelke et al., 1992). They even have an understanding of causality and (im)possibility, manifesting considerable astonishment when two items appear to be inhabiting the same bit of space simultaneously in violation of the laws of physics (Baillargeon et al., 1985; Leslie, 1988).

In the domain of language things are even better: they can keep different languages in their environment separate; they can exploit differences of stress and pitch, and of segmental and syntactic structure; they can discriminate vowel qualities and consonantal contrasts like those distinguishing p and b, t and ʈ, or l and r. They can do this moreover even when the adults around them are singularly unable to do so. At six months, Japanese infants are as good as English ones at distinguishing l and r, but have lost the knack by a year (Jusczyk, 1997). By the same age they have refuted Quine on the issue of the cognitive prerequisites to language acquisition (Soja et al., 1991), and at about two years or so their syntax takes off as they acquire productive mastery of the lexicon of functional categories (Radford, 1990). Then they learn about ten new words a day for the next ten to fifteen years, at which stage they run out of new words and calm down a bit (Bloom, 2000).

This dazzling display, moreover, is not restricted to the odd suckling genius, but is characteristic of essentially every member of the species. Even profoundly deaf children, whose linguistic input is limited to the visual modality, can develop a sign system with the same expressive power as any other natural language. Indeed, both deaf and hearing children seem to be sensitive to the fine detail of the input, whether signed or spoken, by six months of age (Masataka, 1998).

So it is somewhat surprising to read in certain popular publications that you can 'help . . . your baby learn how to talk', 'speed up' its language learning, 'foster communication', 'simplify daily life', and maybe even increase its IQ, by using Baby Signs (Acredolo and Goodwyn, 1996:31–2, 49, 51), a system of non-verbal gestures developed between certain infants and consenting adults. It's surprising, but then so is everything else about infants; so is there any substance to the claims, or is this merely the cynical exploitation of a gullible public by whimsy packaged as science?

It may help to start by highlighting the traditional lay presumption that the acquisition of language is correctly viewed as a process of learning (even of teaching) rather than of natural development. The authors' remark that 'the baby sign experience actually *helps* your baby learn how to talk' (Acredolo and Goodwyn, 1996:49) is not just a momentary aberration, as they talk later of 'the hard work of learning how to string two symbols together' (p. 76). But this is to ignore the radical difference between the maturation of an endogenously controlled system and the laborious mastery of a complex intellectual artefact. Getting to grips with algebra or finding one's way through a maze may be learned (even taught), but when it comes to vision, for instance, no one wishes to claim that we 'learn' to see in three dimensions, even if infants don't develop this ability until the age of sixteen to eighteen weeks. Research of the last few decades has shown that much the same applies to language: as Chomsky memorably put it, 'in certain fundamental respects we do not really learn language; rather, grammar grows in the mind' (1980a:134).

However, not all of language is genetically determined; both an innate base and some environmental input are **necessary** components of the acquisition process. Without some socialization, language acquisition is impossible (Bloom, 2000; Tomasello, 1999), and leaving your child in front of the TV is no substitute for interacting with it. Perhaps early gestures of the sort encouraged by Baby Signs have a contributory effect here, though they certainly have no necessary role. For example, the use of gestures might simply induce the Hawthorne effect (discovered by Elton Mayo in conducting research at the Hawthorne plant of the Western Electric Company in the 1920s). By enlisting the workers' (or babies') co-operation, you stimulate a new more positive attitude, and their productivity (or responsiveness) improves dramatically, irrespective of the nature of the co-operative enterprise. The role of Baby Signs would then be not dissimilar to that of motherese, whose main function is 'to make babies psychologically tolerable rather than linguistically proficient' (Smith, 1989a:153).

It is important not to **over**-estimate the importance of the social dimension. Tomasello (1999) has argued extensively – and plausibly – that language acquisition is based, in part, on social-cognitive processes, specifically the understanding at nine months of others as intentional agents: coming to appreciate that others are 'like me'. But this can only be a (very) small part of the explanation, as the automaticity of language acquisition even in the absence of normal socialization is attested to by the remarkable success of autistic subjects like Donna Williams (1992, 1994, 1996), Temple Grandin (1986) and Liane Willey (1999) in acquiring language.

Assuming that the proponents of Baby Signs are correct in claiming (for instance) a statistically significant IQ advantage for Baby Signers over controls (Acredolo and Goodwyn, 1988; Acredolo, 2000), an explanation of the kind I suggested above seems to be more plausible than their own. Acredolo (2000) claims that the success of Baby Signs arises in large part because they enable the infant to by-pass 'the obstacles posed by the articulatory component of language'. She seems to think that learning a word consists merely in learning how to pronounce it; but articulatory difficulty is not obviously involved in acquiring an auditory (or acoustic or visual) representation for either words or signs. All children can identify words correctly before they can produce them correctly; and in my experience (e.g. Smith, 1973, and chapter 17 below) articulatory difficulties are not significant: children happily tolerate enormous homophony in their own speech, even if they take exception to adults mimicking it in theirs.

Moreover, if articulatory difficulty were a factor, one would expect that the language acquisition of deaf signing children should be in advance of their relatively disadvantaged hearing peers. Although there is evidence that the first signs of deaf children appear before the first words of hearing children (probably because of the earlier maturation of the respective motor systems), it is significant that such early signing does not speed up subsequent development of the language: 'none of the subsequent milestones (e.g. timing of the first two-word utterances) is convincingly earlier in American Sign Language than in speech', as Newport and Meier (1985:889) put it. Further, Nicoladis and her associates (Nicoladis et al., 1999) have shown that early 'representational gestures' (as opposed to signs) are never combined; that gestures that occur before children begin to speak show no correlation with MLU (mean length of utterance); and most strikingly, that the richness of early gesturing in bilingual children brought up speaking English and French correlates with their relative proficiency in the respective language, and not with their cognitive ability.

Acredolo and Goodwyn's book is over-stated, linguistically naive, and should be read with a pinch of salt. If you want a more sober, but equally accessible, assessment of infants' abilities, you could try Annette Karmiloff-Smith's (1994) *Baby it's You*. But this has an equally repellent picture of a baby on the cover, so maybe you should use your common sense and the technical literature. According to the Psalmist (Psalm 8, in case you had forgotten) babes and sucklings have amazing powers: they can even silence enmity and vengeance. That may be a trifle exaggerated, but they certainly have an impressive array of talents, even before their doting parents are inveigled into gesturing at them.

Acknowledgement

This chapter first appeared in 2001 in *Glot International* 5:13–15.

Further reading

Relevant discussion of suckling abilities appears now in Clark (2004).

6

Censored?

Assassination is the extreme form of censorship.
George Bernard Shaw, *The Rejected Statement*

The question mark in the title reflects some doubt as to whether I have really been censored and, if I have, whether the censorship is too trivial to worry about. It is certainly not in the same league as Shaw's example of censorship by assassination, but it may none-theless be significant. Let me explain. I was recently invited to write an encyclopedia article about Chomsky. I was given a couple of hundred words to encapsulate his life, his intellectual contribution, and a brief outline of his political thought. The format was pre-ordained, and I submitted the following:

> **Chomsky, Noam (1928–),** American linguist, philosopher and political activist, revolutionised the study of language with his (transformational) *generative grammar*. Observing that people can pro-duce and understand any of an infinite number of sentences, many of which they have never heard before, he claims that humans are born knowing the principles of Universal Grammar according to which all languages are structured. Hearing the language spoken around them is then sufficient to trigger the linguistic ability that children have from birth. His research program simultaneously resurrected the theory of innate ideas in philosophy, and has been influential in psychology, mathematics, and education.
>
> He is equally known for his writing and lecturing on dissident politics: documenting the lies of government, exposing the hidden influence of big business, and developing a model of the social order which focuses on the role of the media in disseminating propaganda.

This work has had considerable influence on libertarian socialist movements, and has resulted in his being the world's most widely quoted living author.

Avram Noam Chomsky was born in Philadelphia. He graduated from the University of Pennsylvania in 1949, and earned his PhD there in 1955, the same year that he joined the faculty of the Massachusetts Institute of Technology. He has written over 80 books, including: *Syntactic Structures* (1957), *Aspects of the Theory of Syntax* (1965), *American Power and the New Mandarins* (1969), *Reflections on Language* (1975), *Peace in the Middle East?* (1975), *Rules and Representations* (1980), *Lectures on Government and Binding* (1981), *Knowledge of Language* (1986), *Necessary Illusions* (1989), *Deterring Democracy* (1991), *Year 501: The Conquest Continues* (1993), *The Minimalist Program* (1995), *Powers and Prospects: Reflections on Human Nature and the Social Order* (1996), and *New Horizons in the Study of Language and Mind* (2000).

I received a polite note saying 'Thanks so much for your work on the article! I just glanced at it and it looks great.' I also received $60.00. Six months later I received a progress report, saying that my article had 'been routed through our staff of editors and fact-checkers, and I have included the newest version below for your final approval. It has been edited slightly for length, research findings, and for consistency.'

This was the slightly edited version:

Chomsky, Noam (1928–), is an American linguist, philosopher, and political activist. He revolutionized the study of language with his introduction of generative grammar, also called transformational grammar. Generative grammar consists of rules that determine all the sentences that can possibly be formed in any language. Chomsky claimed that human beings possess this knowledge at birth. His research has influenced theories of innate (inborn) ideas in philosophy, as well as psychology, mathematics, and education.

Chomsky is also known for his political beliefs, many of which disagree with the people who hold power. His lectures and writings have sought to expose what he views as government lies and the hidden influence of big business. Chomsky's work has influenced socialist movements that favor limiting government activities.

Avram Noam Chomsky was born in Philadelphia. He graduated from the University of Pennsylvania in 1949, and he earned his Ph.D. there in 1955. Chomsky joined the faculty of the Massachusetts Institute of Technology later that year. He has written more than

80 books and is a widely quoted author. Some of his books include *Syntactic Structures* (1957); *Aspects of the Theory of Syntax* (1965); *Reflections on Language* (1975); *Lectures on Government and Binding* (1981); *Deterring Democracy* (1991); and *New Horizons in the Study of Language and Mind* (2000).

So they saved seventy-eight words, mainly by abbreviating the list of references. Fair enough; even if the selection was a little biased: Chomsky has written more books on politics than on linguistics. However, they also got his linguistics wrong: to the extent that their characterization makes sense, it sounds like a description of E-language rather than I-language, and the innateness claim is simplistic to the point of caricature. Moreover, it's strictly speaking false: as pointed out elsewhere (Smith, 2004:30), Chomsky has repeatedly said that the aim for exhaustive coverage is radically misguided. The second paragraph is no better. Apart from the gruesome style, which has beliefs disagreeing with people, the remark about 'lies' has been carefully given downgraded 'evidentiality' (Rooryck, 2001), and 'propaganda' has disappeared entirely: surprising, given the title of his most recent book (Chomsky, 2001). Maybe this is all trivial. Certainly, my experience does not come in the same league as that of many others, and the sanitizing carried out for 'space and objectivity concerns', as they charmingly put it, is insignificant beside many other cases. I will digress for a moment.

Over the years, the study of language has been marked by a number of unsavoury episodes, ranging from the mildly dispiriting, like the foul-mouthed polemics of the 'linguistics wars' documented by Harris (1993) and Newmeyer (1980:162), to the iniquitously bizarre. The most notorious is perhaps the dominance in Soviet linguistics of the ideas of Nikolay Yakovlevich Marr. Marr believed that 'language is conditioned by social and economic factors' – an 'axiom which it was not permitted to doubt' (Ivic, 1965:105) – and that all languages developed from a stock of four elements, *sal, ber, yon* and *rosh*, in keeping with the changes in socio-economic development of their speakers. For years, he and his ludicrous ideas were supported by Stalin, and all opposing views were suppressed until, in a moment of rationality, the dictator observed that the Russian of Pushkin and the tsars wasn't all that different from the Russian of the Soviets, and Marrism fell from favour. Ludicrous, but devastating for those who disagreed, who could lose their livelihoods, even their lives.

Another miserable event revolves around Roman Jakobson. Apparently his arrival in the United States in 1941 was not uniformly welcomed and a group of linguists mailed him 'a dollar bill bearing their signatures and suggesting that he use the dollar as a down payment on a return ticket to Europe at the earliest feasible moment' (Halle, 1988:738, fn.2). This kind of attempted censorship is simply iniquitous and, if possible, to be opposed.

Chomsky himself is no stranger to censorship of his political writings. In 'A prefatory note by the authors on the history of the suppression of the first edition of this book', Chomsky and Herman (1979:xiv–xvii) report how their monograph on relations between the United States and the Third World was suppressed by its publisher's parent company. They comment further that such an episode and the indifference with which it was met 'reflect the importance of the selective policing of the flow of ideas by means of private structures' (1979:xvi). There are all sorts of possible reactions, from outrage to indifference. One common response is that all choice involves censorship of alternatives. But such censorship of ideas is distinct from the epiphenomenal censorship that we all indulge in when we appoint a Functionalist rather than a Formalist to our latest departmental vacancy; or decide to limit the field of job applicants to morphologists rather than syntacticians next time we hire someone; or even when we persuade our students to work on Optimality Theory rather than Government phonology.

To return to my own minor brush with the 'selective policing of the flow of ideas', I think that, however marginal the context (or the encyclopedia), it is important to get the details right and to let people say or write what they want to. Even though the upshot of my withdrawing my contribution will probably be that an even less enlightening, or enlightened, version of 'Chomsky' is published instead; and even if it seems that I am seeing monsters under beds where there are scarcely even beds, let alone monsters, all censorship must be fought. However 'trivial', such behaviour by a company which claims that 'since 1917 [it] has set the standard for providing accuracy, objectivity, and reliability in research materials' is inherently unacceptable: hence the above. Enough is enough.

As a postscript, it should be mentioned that I claim no definitive status of 'validity' for my overly laconic summary of Chomsky, or even for my slightly longer book (Smith, 2004), and it would be interesting to see what the community of linguists came up with if asked to summarize in a single sentence his major claim to inclusion in a general encyclopedia. In fact, subject to the editors' approval, I suggest that everyone send in a completion (in no more than twenty words) of the sentence 'Chomsky is important because . . .'. Then the most interesting/representative/original . . . could be published in a future issue of *Glot International*. Uncensored.

Acknowledgement

A version of this chapter first appeared in 2001 in *Glot International* 5:311–13.

Further reading

See now Postal's 'Policing the content of linguistic examples' (in press: ch.15).
As *Glot International* is now defunct, I will put all such submissions on my web page.

7

Did you Know that the Portuguese for Turkey is Peru?

Meleagris gallopavo

No, they're not geographically confused; rather, the Portuguese word for the fowl that carnivores tend to eat at Christmas or Thanksgiving is 'peru'. I suspect that the Portuguese are as misguided as the English about the origin of the bird, as in many other languages some reference to 'India' features in the name, but never mind. Purveying such gobbets of information is mildly entertaining and amuses the lay audience, even if it reinforces the view that linguists predominantly study etymology and the idiosyncrasies of meaning and change of meaning. But then it risks being pernicious if this encourages people to go away with the idea that linguistics is about such facts rather than ideas, about anecdotes rather than theories. One of the major achievements of the generative enterprise has been to lead us away from a situation where erudition can be a substitute for thought. Some knowledge of the facts in any domain is obviously a prerequisite to constructive theorizing, but such knowledge is the beginning not the end.

There is no harm in regaling your friends with linguistic titbits: that 'glamour' and 'grammar' are etymologically the same; that the Thai for 'pork' is, disconcertingly, 'moo'; that the Hindi for 'Grandma' is 'Daddy' (actually just 'paternal Grandma', and really [da:di:]); that the Welsh for 'good' and 'sober' are 'mad' and 'sad' respectively; that the Nupe for 'eye' is 'eye'. As with the turkey, this last equivalence is not quite what it seems – the Nupe is pronounced [ejé], and is only tonally distinct from the word for 'nose', which is [ejè] (so this is only an eye-rhyme) – but it certainly intrigues Nupe children when they learn English. There is no harm, as long as people are not misled into thinking that these trivia are the domain of central concern – theory construction: a realm that fails to include etymology and the associated field of semantic change.

We know that words can extend their meaning (as with 'paper' from 'papyrus'), or narrow their meaning (as with 'deer' from the Old English 'deor' – German 'Tier' – meaning 'animal', which in turn means 'a breathing creature'), or just change their meaning (as evident in such etymological doublets as 'potion' and 'poison'). Learned scholars can then produce collections of such examples and speculate freely about the psychology of the speakers of the various languages; they can write whole books on the etymology of 'ginger' (Ross, 1952), or compile surveys of other people's suggestions (e.g. Ullmann, 1959). But this is not science. Now non-science is not the same as non-sense, and it is clear from the work of Traugott and Dasher (2002), for instance, that there are general, perhaps universal, tendencies in semantic change, and that these can be plausibly attributed to the role of 'invited inferences' and the exploitation of metonymy. Crucially, however, such accounts are not predictive, make no testable hypotheses, and by such criteria remain non-scientific. The implication is that this is not a domain for theory construction, and is ultimately sterile.

Assuming that we wish to avoid such sterility, two questions immediately arise. First, why do people like these factoids so much? Second, what is a respectable alternative? The answer to the first is, probably, because it obviates the need for thought; the answer to the second is an explanatory theory of (I-)language. Given Saussurean arbitrariness and the notorious lack of constraints on our ability to construct free mental associations, there is unlikely to be a predictive theory of the relation between sound and meaning, and hence no theory of the relations between word meanings over time. But when it comes to the computational system of the language faculty, things are different; theories can flourish, and falsifiable predictions are legion.

Let's go back to the title. Interestingly, this question is ungrammatical for some speakers, because it contains a sequence of tense violation. For such people the correct form would have to be: 'Did you know that the Portuguese for TURKEY <u>was</u> PERU?' There is in fact some dialectal and idiosyncratic variation: for me, the form with 'was' is normal (see chapter 12 for discussion), while the form with 'is' is also well-formed but has the additional connotation that I accept responsibility for the truth of the embedded clause; for others, this second possibility doesn't exist, and the title as given is simply impossible. But now we have an area where it makes sense to ask for principled explanations and there are indeed several explicit theories of (sequence of) tense that we can appeal to(e.g. Reichenbach, 1947; Comrie, 1985, 1986; Declerck, 1991; Hornstein, 1990).

These competing theories are in parts incompatible, but there is one particular aspect of their accounts of the phenomenon that is relevant here, and where they are probably in tacit agreement: the relation they postulate between syntax proper and the rest of the language faculty. It is a commonplace that the interpretation of utterances involves both a stage internal to the grammar and a variety of stages beyond the grammar. That is, the grammar specifies a level of representation (LF, to take a specific case) which captures the purely syntactic properties of sentences, and then semantic and pragmatic processes enrich and modify this representation to give a fully interpreted propositional form. For current purposes, the technical details of how this is implemented are irrelevant, as long as we have a distinction between LF and (e.g.) LF′ (pronounced 'LF-prime'), where, by hypothesis, LF is a level of representation within the grammar, and LF′ is a level of representation dependent on processes external to the grammar. The claim is that the characterization of sequence of tense then crucially involves LF′; that is, it falls in part outside core syntax. In fact, the various theories of tense I have mentioned are not always crystal-clear on the division of responsibility between what is inside and what is outside the grammar. Hornstein claims explicitly that LF′ is the correct locus for the treatment of sequence of tense, but he actually makes his version of LF′ part of 'the structure of the grammar' (1990:233); Comrie emphasizes that sequence of tense is a 'purely formal operation' (1986:290) – that is, it is part of the syntax proper, but nonetheless he is equally explicit about the need 'to distinguish between meaning and interpretation' (1985:111); and Declerck, whose treatment is the most comprehensive and persuasive, argues (1991:188) for the need to use Gricean implicatures – hence for devices outside the syntax proper; but it is not clear that any of these scholars would accept the demarcation I am proposing.

Be that as it may; to illustrate the current point, what is important is that we have a theory that makes this particular distinction and therefore makes specific predictions. Consider the polyglot savant Christopher, whom Ianthi Tsimpli and I have been studying for the last decade or so (most recently with added help – see Morgan et al., 2002). In our earlier work (Tsimpli and Smith, 1993; Smith and Tsimpli, 1995) we have documented the fact that Christopher's English syntax is normal across a huge range of constructions; but we also noted that there was one domain – dislocation and topicalization constructions – where his judgements deviated from those of normal native speakers.

Although he had normal intuitions about the acceptability of – among other things – relative clauses, embedded interrogatives, *easy-to-please* constructions, parasitic gaps and clefts, he judged all the examples in (1) to be ill-formed:

1a.   Steven, they saw during the break
  b.   Me, I don't like football
  c.   I met her yesterday, Mary

We accounted for this surprising deviation by arguing that such constructions crucially involved not just the grammar, but also a level of representation, LF′, beyond the grammar – appealing to processes of the central system. As we had systematically argued that Christopher had an intact grammar but an impaired central system, we were then able to maintain our claim that his syntactic competence was indeed normal, and that the reason for his abnormal judgements was a function of the role of the (impaired) central system.

The argument was, and is, controversial, and may turn out to be wrong; but if it is correct, it makes the prediction that Christopher might well have problems with any other construction involving the postulated level of representation LF′. That is, there should be a natural class of all and only those phenomena involving LF′. And sure enough there was one other area where Christopher's English intuitions differed from ours: (sequence of) tenses. Thus, he consistently judged examples like (2a) as 'incorrect' and replaced them with examples like (2b):

2a.   The defendant denied that he takes hashish
  b.   The defendant denied that he took hashish

Of course, this example alone simply suggests that Christopher belongs to the dialect in which (2a) (and the title of this column) are ungrammatical; but other examples of his reaction to tense phenomena belied this interpretation. For instance, he seemed systematically to implement a strategy of tense harmony either between a tense inflection and a temporal adverbial, or between two tense inflections, changing the fully acceptable examples in (3) to their congeners in (4):

3a.   It is time that we left for Newcastle
  b.   Fred left tomorrow according to the original plan
  c.   Tom heard that his friend was coming tomorrow

4a.   It is time that we leave for Newcastle
  b.   Fred will leave tomorrow according to the original plan
  c.   Tom heard that his friend will be coming tomorrow

As (4c) is ungrammatical for those who speak the 'strict' sequence of tense variety of English, his divergent judgements cannot simply be the result of a dialect difference, but rather reflect the same problem with interactions between the grammar and the interpretive (central) system that we had seen with the dislocation examples.

Many of the steps in this argument are contentious, but the beauty of couching the discussion in the framework of a theory is that it allows one to make predictions and test them out: here the surprising claim that sequence of tense and topicalization phenomena form a natural class. Even if the particular examples turn out to be analysed better in some other way, it is clear that we have here a proper domain for theory construction, unlike the inherently anecdotal areas of etymology and sound–meaning correspondence in the lexicon. Collecting such trivial examples as those we started with is harmless, but it doesn't lead anywhere. Theories lead you into making unexpected and testable claims. The interesting part of the title really resides in the choice of *is* rather than *was*, not in the Portuguese for 'turkey'.

Oh and by the way – did you know that the Turkish for 'turkey' is 'Hindi'?

Acknowledgement

This chapter appeared originally in 2002 in *Glot International* 6:91–3.

Part II

Language in the Genes

8

Obstinacy

He was a linguist, and therefore he had pushed the bounds of obstinacy well beyond anything that is conceivable to other men.

Helen de Witt, *The Last Samurai*

There used to be a fashion for 'irregular verbs':

I have preferences	You have biases	He has prejudices.
I am frugal	You are stingy	He is a cheapskate.
I am sparkling	You are unusually talkative	He is drunk.

Of these I have always felt attracted to:

I am firm-willed	You are obstinate	He is pig-headed.

I think that there is a lot to be said for obstinacy. There is an unhealthy tendency to assume that it is necessarily allied to irrationality, at least when it is predicated of other people. This is unhelpful, as obstinacy and irrationality are not necessarily linked. There is of course plentiful evidence for associating the two: consider the archetypal form of irrational credulousness seen in the attention paid to astrology and the influence on life of one's star sign. Astrology is bunk. It is true that one sometimes sees quoted as evidence for the rationality of such superstition the observation that, for instance, the incidence of schizophrenia correlates – statistically significantly – with birth date. How about that for cast-iron evidence of the validity of astrology and the sensibleness of gazing at your horoscope? Well, not very good actually: a more plausible explanation – that is, one where the causal mechanism is transparent as opposed to mystic – is that schizophrenia is caused (in part) by enlargement of the ventricles of the brain due to deficient ultra-violet light during development (Furlow, 2001). The incidence of UV light is, of course, correlated with time of year, which, in turn, correlates with star sign. But the effect of Saturn (or Venus or whatever) is still (so far as we know) zero. This will not stop the gullible from continuing to believe the twaddle peddled by horoscopists, but it does give the rational a suitable reply to their maunderings.

In fact, rationality and obstinacy (doubly) dissociate, and obstinacy can be a useful trait, characterizing both the bizarre interests of the autistic savant, who may spend countless hours performing calculations to estimate on what day of the week 3 August 2088 falls (Tuesday, in case you're wondering); and the (perhaps no less bizarre) preoccupations of Nobel laureates, who may spend countless hours in the 'time-intensive, fanatical concentration' (Gleick, 1992:382) their creative but esoteric work requires.

Such obsessions are treated as rational if they yield a Nobel prize; irrational if they merely give rise to obscure publications in minor journals, or (in the case of the savant) to a sophisticated peep-show. And this even though the latter's obsession may be the one means of gaining both intellectual satisfaction and some attention from an otherwise uncomprehending and often equally incomprehensible public. In some cases the obsessive obstinacy may be fuelled by love and devotion of a more understandable kind. In an alternately inspiring and horrifying book (Hale, 2002), Sheila Hale documents the effects of a catastrophic stroke on her art historian husband, showing simultaneously the severity and the partialness of his loss. In a clear case of modular dissociation, his esthetic appreciation appeared to have been left unaffected, even though his language faculty was essentially wiped out. Her obstinacy in overcoming a catalogue of appalling ignorance and prejudice in an attempt to find some remedy for his condition was dismissed as irrational by some members of the medical profession, and her efforts were sadly rewarded only in part, as her husband died without regaining appreciable mastery of language.

The moral to be drawn from such examples is that obstinacy may be good or bad, rational or irrational, varying from case to case.

The crucial variable is whether you have evidence for the position you are defending. If you do, and if that evidence is persuasive enough, it will enable you to defend your position against apparent falsification. Indeed, obstinate attempts to provide rational explanations for the apparently irrational may be sufficient to help eliminate the naivety from 'naive falsificationism' in the sense of Lakatos (1970). Lakatos argued that the Popperian criterion of falsifiability was too simplistic. Rational people do not give up theories which have the power to explain a host of disparate facts simply because there are data that contradict them. As Chomsky has repeatedly emphasized (e.g. 1980b:2), theories are not falsified by observational data; a hypothesis spawned by a theory may be refuted, so that that hypothesis is given up, but the obstinate defence of apparently 'falsified' theories is part of the essence of science, when science is construed as aiming to explain a little rather than describe a lot.

Mention of Chomsky reminds me that he is obstinate (and rational). Consider as an example his position on innateness over the last forty-five years or so. As early as in his review of Skinner's *Verbal Behavior* he observed that language acquisition must take place 'through genetically determined maturation' (1959:564), and that even though 'we cannot yet describe or begin to understand' how this happens, the processes 'may be largely innate' (p. 563). Not everyone was convinced, especially not philosophers such as Goodman, Putnam and Quine. A few years later, in *Aspects*, Chomsky elaborated his views with the observation that

> a consideration of the character of the grammar that is acquired, the degenerate quality and narrowly limited extent of the available data, the striking uniformity of the resulting grammars, and their independence of intelligence, motivation, and emotional state, over wide ranges of variation, leave little hope that much of the structure of language can be learned by an organism initially uninformed as to its general character. (1965:58)

Still not everyone was convinced. In 1975, discussing the 'innateness hypothesis' (IH), he writes that 'some intellectual achievements, such as language learning, fall strictly within biologically determined cognitive capacity' for which we have 'special design' (1975:27). By this time, the language acquisition literature was itself burgeoning, providing more and more evidence for the nature of what must be innate; but not everyone was convinced. In the 1980s he returned to the fray, arguing that 'biological endowment sharply constrains the course of language growth' (1980a:232), and elsewhere he anticipated that it would turn out more generally that 'human cognitive capacities are highly structured by our genetic program' (Peck, 1987:199; originally from 1976), even though he embedded this observation in a carefully hedged conditional about the differences among human abilities.

To make the limitations of 'learning' more obvious, and to accentuate the role of genetic determination, Chomsky wrote whimsically: 'I am personally quite convinced that no matter what training or education I might have received, I could never have run a four-minute mile, discovered Gödel's theorems, composed a Beethoven quartet, or risen to any of innumerable other heights of human achievement. I feel in no way demeaned by these inadequacies' (Peck, 1987:198). Reactions remained intermittently hostile, and the saga continued as he reiterated that the initial state of the language faculty is 'genetically determined' (1995a:14), or 'the language organ is like others in that its basic character is an expression of the genes' (2000a:4). Even more recently, in a reply to Alison Gopnik, he writes (2003:316): 'There has been a great deal of controversy about IH, but with an oddly one-sided character. IH has been sharply criticized, but it has never been formulated or defended. True, specific proposals have been made about innateness.' Chomsky must have returned to this particular issue a hundred times over the years, rebutting each naive counter-example in turn. More importantly, in the form of the Principles and Parameters framework, he and his followers have fulfilled the essential task of providing the most detailed and explicit proposals about what precisely is innate. The quotes I have given above are not just idle promissory notes. The thesis may of course be wrong, but that just means that it is an empirical claim.

If one has an idea, most people are content with publishing it, and seeing it taken note of; even if only by refutation. It takes considerable firmness of will, obstinacy, pig-headedness to return to its defence again and again and again, the way Chomsky has. And that is at least in part why, even though they are still attacked, (some of) his ideas have gradually taken on the aura of orthodoxy: the claim that some considerable portion of the human language faculty is 'innate' no longer raises eyebrows, even if it continues to fuel disagreement.

So Chomsky is rationally obstinate, but if you want real obstinacy, turn to a two-year-old. I have been observing my grandson, Zachary, now 2 years and 2 months, and trying to work out some of the details of his language development. Last week I wanted specific data on his phonology, as he seemed to be pronouncing the initial elements of *Grandma* and *Grandpa* unexpectedly differently. Having failed to elicit the required examples by the usual stealth, I resorted in desperation to direct questioning. The conversation went as follows:

NS	Can you say 'Grandma'?	Z	[ræma:]
NS	Can you say 'Grandpa'?	Z	no. (Uttered with a mischievous smile)
NS	Can you say 'no'?	Z	no no.
NS	Can you say 'no no'?	Z	no no no.
NS	Can you say 'no no no'?	Z	no no no no.
NS	Can you say 'no no no no'?	Z	no! (vehemently)

So I know he can count, but I'm still not sure how he pronounces me.

As for me, I shall go on obstinately writing columns for *Glot* even though it will no longer exist after this issue – it's been too much fun to stop. Maybe I'm irrational, but thank you for having me anyway.

Acknowledgement

This chapter appeared in 2003 as my final column for *Glot International* (7:244–6) before it ceased publication.

Further reading

Further examples from Zachary can be found in the postscript to chapter 17 below. Chomsky discusses innateness yet again in his (2004).

9

Backlash

What could possibly be innate?
Title of a 1971 paper by John Morton

UG or not UG, that is the question.

The faculty of language 'is some kind of expression of the genes' (Chomsky, 2000a:187), hence our knowledge of language is, in part, innately determined. Who could possibly disagree? Well, lots of people actually. The last few years have seen a powerful empiricist backlash against this nativist position, with sustained attempts to refute or undermine many of the arguments that have been deployed over the years in its defence. It's time to take stock: some of the arguments are silly or tendentious, and some have a certain initial plausibility that tends to evaporate on closer examination, but there is nonetheless a residue that demands serious attention.

I will start by listing ten or so of the best-known arguments for an innate component to language; then look at some of the contrary literature, including some rather blatant red herrings; and finally highlight one or two of the substantive issues.

Evidence for there being properties of the 'initial state' of the human infant that predispose it to acquire language comes in at least the following categories:

- **Universals**: both of adult grammars and the stages of their acquisition by children.
- The **poverty of the stimulus**: we end up knowing more than we can plausibly have extracted from the input to us; striking examples are provided by intuitions of ill-formedness.

- The **speed and age-dependence** of first language acquisition, suggesting that it is subject to one or more 'critical periods'.
- The **convergence** among grammars of speakers who differ greatly in other putatively relevant attributes. An obvious example is provided by linguistically normal pathological populations, such as Williams syndrome children, whose impaired intelligence puts a greater burden on the innate component than in the 'normal' population.
- The **species-specificity** of the language faculty.
- The **heritability** of some language disorders, such as developmental dyslexia and Specific Language Impairment (SLI). The KE family (Gopnik and Crago, 1991) provides the clearest example.
- The **domain-specificity** of problem-solving behaviour. Smith and Tsimpli (1995) demonstrated that structure-independent operations were impossible to learn within the language faculty, even when subjects were capable of solving the same problem in a different cognitive domain.
- The existence of **emergent categories**. Eve Clark (2001) has argued that children's lexical over-extensions, whereby 'moon' in English, for instance, is generalized to a variety of other round objects, reflect the availability of conceptual categories (shape, in this case) which are manifest in the classifier systems of a variety of languages, even though they do not show up in English.
- If they exist, **parametric cascades** or **major parameters** (in the sense of Holmberg and Sandström, 1996) are further evidence in favour of UG; and there is an *a priori* argument in Jerry Fodor's (1975) avoidance of an infinite regress in his 'language of thought' hypothesis.

All these arguments have been impugned, with varying degrees of plausibility, by *inter alia* Bates and Elman (1996) and a wide range of connectionists; Culicover (1999); Sampson (1999); and Tomasello (2000a, 2000b). The most sustained, yet least successful, counter-blast comes from Sampson. In a distasteful critique he mounts attacks on many of the arguments listed above. He claims that the argument from speed of acquisition (*vis-à-vis* the acquisition of knowledge of physics, for instance) is meaningless unless quantified, or constitutes 'hand-waving' (1999:36), because Chomsky also claims that even knowledge of physics depends on innate properties of mind. Given the gross disparity between the time it takes children to learn their first language and the time it takes linguists to characterize the children's knowledge, quantification is irrelevant. The crucial point is that **all** of our abilities are under-pinned by innate structures; **some** of them are underpinned by **dedicated** innate structures, often referred to as 'modules', a notion that Sampson ignores. Modularity hypotheses of various flavours provide a simple account of a range of facts, including the double dissociations characteristic of much pathology. The age-dependence of acquisition likewise receives short shrift: all learning is supposedly done better in childhood, and the difference between first and second language acquisition can be attributed to 'motivation'. That all children learn their first language perfectly and only rather few adults achieve comparable mastery of a sec-ond is left unexplained. The evidence for critical periods and from dissociations is somewhat better than Sampson suggests, as I have pointed out earlier (Smith, 1998a, 1998b).

The last and most important of the arguments he attacks is the poverty of the stimulus. Sampson argues that evidence for structure-dependence, for instance, is plentiful in the input, and that there is accordingly **no** poverty of the stimulus. Chomsky's rhetorical claim that you could go through much of your life without hearing relevant evidence is probably exaggerated, but Sampson's choice of counter-examples is remarkable, including sentences from the *Wall Street Journal*, and William Blake's poem 'Tiger'. This latter has the line 'Did he who made the lamb make thee?', which is nicely parallel to Chomsky's 'Is the man who is tall in the room?' However, the argument is hardly cogent, as children are normally exposed to such literature only after they have fixed all the relev-ant parameters; and if they did pay close attention to Blake's poem, they would be in trouble: a few lines earlier comes the couplet: 'In what distant deeps or skies / Burnt the fire of thine eyes?' – cast-iron evidence that English allows V to I movement for main verbs.

If Sampson is snide, Bates and Elman are disingenuous. On the basis of a somewhat simplistic reading, they assert that Saffran et al. (1996) 'have proven that babies can learn', which 'flies in the face of received wisdom . . . [as] Noam Chomsky . . . has argued for forty years that language is unlearnable' (Bates and Elman, 1996:1849–50). There are many problems with this claim. First, all sane people (which I take it includes Chomsky) admit that language acquisition has both a learned and an innate component. Second, while some aspects of language **use** are clearly dependent on such (statistical) matters as word frequency, there is little evidence that the rules of the grammar reflect those statistics, or even that Saffran's experiments were tapping the language faculty. More importantly, connectionist networks are too proficient at statistics for their own good: as mentioned above (and see Smith, 1997), humans appear to be unable to use in the linguistic domain counting techniques that they can deploy easily in a puzzle-solving cognitive domain.

Let us turn to a more cogent and coherent critic. Michael Tomasello has been arguing for some years in favour of a 'usage-based' approach to first language acquisition, and against the continuity hypothesis of UG. He characterizes children's language 'not in terms of innate, adult-like, formal grammars, but rather in terms of the cognitive and communicative processes involved' (Tomasello, 2000b:161). While this last locution may not be entirely transparent, it appears to mean that whatever properties characterize the young language learner, they are not specific to language, but rather domain-general. As a consequence, children show no evidence of syntactic categories (except noun) in the early stages of acquisition, and fail to over-generalize, until such time as their maturing cognition enables them to create syntactic categories by a general process of induction. Apart from the question of whether induction can really solve the problem of syntactic acquisition (he deals only with argument structure), there are several problems with Tomasello's account. For instance, he has no account of how we come by intuitions of ill-formedness; much of his evidence on the unevenness of the development of categories is **not** inconsistent with most generative theories; and many of his arguments just fail to go through. For instance, he suggests that when 'children began to use the determiners *a* and *the* between 2 and 3 years of age, they did so with almost completely different sets of nouns . . . This suggested that the children at this age did not have any kind of abstract category of determiner' (2000b:157; cf. 2000a:214). But if *a* occurs with N_1 to N_i, and *the* occurs with N_j to N_m, and neither occurs with adjectives or verbs or prepositions (whether or not these are themselves well-defined categories), this seems precisely to suggest that there are (at least) two classes: nouns of different kinds, and things that can occur with them – 'determiners'? In brief, I don't think his arguments work, but his careful research raises serious problems for 'strong continuity', even if not for maturational theories, and simultaneously highlights the difficulty of deciding which properties of the initial state are specific to language and which are a function of general cognition.

And the opposition's arguments are getting better. Some of the best are presented in Peter Culicover's intriguing book *Syntactic Nuts*. He proposes that a 'Conservative, Attentive Learner' can learn his or her first language, with no need to appeal to principles or parameters, by induction over the input. The focus of his argument and the bulk of his evidence come from the eponymous syntactic nuts: irregular or partially irregular constructions which – despite their peripheral status – give rise to intuitions among native speakers of comparable robustness to those arising from the mastery of the core of the language. The argument continues that, as these idiosyncratic constructions must be **learned** rather than triggered, and on the parsimonious assumption that there is only one learning mechanism for syntax, the regulars must be assimilated to the periphery. The conclusion is that UG is minimal, and as a corollary we need to revert to using an evaluation measure à la *Aspects* to choose among possible grammars.

Many of Culicover's particular analyses – from *'no matter'* constructions to parasitic gaps – are convincing but, as Janet Fodor (2001) points out in a perceptive review, there are also serious problems with his position. First, like Tomasello, he has no convincing account of intuitions of ill-formedness; second, his assumption that the 'core/periphery' distinction is central to current linguistics (rather than an admission of ignorance) is suspect: assimilating the core to the periphery actually makes different predictions about the errors children will make during the acquisition process; and third, his attempt to claim that the descriptive apparatus (HPSG-type features) and the theory using them should be dissociated is an instrumentalist denial of psychological realism. But he has raised two very significant challenges: one is much the same as Tomasello's claim about domain-generality: we have no justification in assuming that what is innate is specific to language; the second is that we need to reflect further on the assignment of duties as between the learning theory and the grammar: for Culicover, the theory of markedness which constitutes (part of) the evaluation measure belongs to the former, not the latter. If he is right, the innate **linguistic** component is again minimized.

So, is UG or isn't UG? Many of the attacks on it are half-baked, and many others, such as arguments from neural localization, or from the plasticity of the brain, or the achievements of bonobos, or the mere existence of a language of thought, are either irrelevant or neutral. So the answer is: definitely UG; but Culicover's and Tomasello's work means that in future we will need to be a little more scrupulous in precisely what we claim about it.

Acknowledgement

This chapter first appeared in 2001 in *Glot International* 5:169–71.

Further reading

Annabel Cormack (p.c.) has suggested that, in the Minimalist Program, UG is no longer a relevant concept, as the intricacies of the core syntax are epiphenomena arising from the '"design specifications" of external systems' (Chomsky, 2000b:94). If this strong minimalist hypothesis turns out to be correct, there is a sense in which she is right. However, the discovery that the principles of UG were deducible from other properties of the mind would give us rich insight into that, and the intricate patterns of variation which are characteristic of different languages, and which are captured by parametric variation, would still need to be accounted for. For relevant discussion, see Hauser et al. (2002) and Collins (2004).

For discussion of 'the child's contribution to language learning', in particular in the context of statistical learning, see now Lidz and Gleitman (2004).

Useful discussion of the debate on the role of statistics in language acquisition can be found in Yang (2004).

For recent discussion of dyslexia, see, for instance, Ramus et al. (2003).

The claimed double dissociation of language abilities in various pathological conditions, specifically SLI and Williams Syndrome, is also a matter of controversy; see Stojanovik et al. (2004).

The debate on UG is continued in chapter 11.

10

Is There a Gene for Linguists?

An odd interest, dependent, I suspect, on some rather kinky gene which, fortunately for our species, is not very widely distributed in the population.

Roger Brown, *A First Language*

There has been heated discussion in the literature on whether there is a 'gene for language'. Anyone who has taken even a cursory interest in that debate will know that the question is simplistic. There couldn't conceivably be just one gene for language. The language faculty is much too complex to be fully determined by the totality of our genes, let alone a single gene. And anyway there is rarely a single gene for anything – for any single phenotype: genes code for proteins, and these proteins can have a bewildering array of complex effects of various kinds. For instance, consider the pathological condition known as 'fragile X syndrome', which is the most common cause of inherited mental retardation. Apart from their intellectual disability, those who suffer from it are also characterized by having prominent ears and large testicles. This triple of characteristics is not an obvious natural class, and highlights the implausibility of finding one-to-one correlations between the phenotype and (damage to) genes. Looking for a gene for language is a bit like looking for a single cause for a car crash. Failure to apply the brakes, the slippery condition of the road, the tiredness of the drivers, the distracting noise from the passengers, the ambient light could all be implicated. The list is potentially endless and suggesting a unique cause is unlikely to do justice to what happens in the real world.

The complexity of the relation between language and genetics is highlighted by consideration of the development of FOXP2 and the KE family, as illuminatingly described by Marcus and Fisher (2003). Over a period of three generations about half the members of the KE family have suffered from a severe speech and language disorder (for a brief overview see Smith, 2004:131–3). It has been clear for several years that the epidemiological evidence leads to the inevitable conclusion that the problem is genetic in origin, but it was only in 2001 that the nature of that genetic defect was (partially) unravelled. There is now considerable excitement in the field since the discovery that the language problems of the KE family can apparently be attributed to a mutation in a single gene known as FOXP2. This gene was previously known as SPCH1, but was renamed when sequencing revealed the presence of a 'Forkhead bOX' domain within the gene ('P2' just indicates that it was the second gene to be identified on the P branch of a whole family of forkhead genes). Forkhead genes were first identified in fruit-flies, and the name comes from the unusual structures found in fly embryos with mutations in that first gene.

Although attention has been concentrated on the effect of this mutation on the development of language and, in particular, on its putative role in Specific Language Impairment (SLI), the function of FOXP2 is not simple. It acts as a transcription factor that regulates the amount of a particular protein that is produced, which in turn has a cascade effect that influences the amount of other proteins in the cell. Comparison with other, better-known, transcription factors suggests that FOXP2 may affect the mobilization of hundreds – perhaps thousands – of other genes 'downstream', and thereby have an effect on the lungs, the heart and the gut, as well as the central nervous system. In the circumstances, what is surprising is that the problem caused by a mutation in FOXP2 should, apparently, be largely restricted to the speech and language domain. Indeed, Newbury and Monaco (2002:699–700) argue that 'it is unlikely that FOXP2 represents a major gene locus in the onset of language impairment', though 'it is feasible that another gene within the FOXP2 pathway will be involved in the SLI phenotype'.

The problems get murkier when we look at other creatures. FOX genes in general are only found in animals and fungi, so we are unlikely to be talking to plants in the near future, even though our interactions with mushrooms may improve (see Smith, 2001).

Realistically, we also won't be talking to the other animals that share the gene with us. Mice have a version of FOXP2 (see Enard et al., 2002), though its role in our rodent relatives is presumably not a linguistic one. Interestingly, it turns out that chimpanzees are closer to mice than they are to humans with regard to their endowment with FOXP2. But pleiotropy is pervasive, so the wide variety of the potential effects of any gene makes it unsurprising that we share some features with chimps and others with anything from mice to mushrooms.

So the idea that there might be 'a gene for language' is hopeless, but there is clearly a sense in which damage to or loss of a single gene can have effects which show up pre-eminently in one domain. As Chomsky put it (2002b:230) with regard to his inability to understand 'dialectics', 'maybe I've got a gene missing or something'. Well, maybe the dialectic gene is missing, but he appears to have lots of others; in particular, he's got the gene for linguists. It's well known that Chomsky's father William was himself a distinguished linguist, the author of *Hebrew: The Eternal Language* and a variety of other works on classical Semitic philology. This seems to point to the existence of a genetic predisposition to linguistics. Chomsky is not just an isolated example. Members of the linguistic community are bound to be familiar with the seminal work of Paul Kiparsky, but they may not be aware that he too is the son of a distinguished linguist, Valentin Kiparsky, author of numerous works including a Russian historical grammar (1979) and an essay on the etymology of 'walrus' (1952). The Kiparskys too have the linguist gene. And that's not all. Sten Vikner, best known as the author of a 1995 monograph on Germanic, and a wealth of other works, is also the son of a distinguished Romanist and computational linguist: Carl Vikner. Indeed, they have even published jointly (Vikner and Vikner, 1997), a sure sign of genes at work. As an aside, I should point out that I have also published jointly with my elder son (Smith and Smith, 1988), so the Vikners are far from unique, and they and the Smiths also presumably have this gene. In case I have been giving the impression that this gene is sexist, I should emphasize that it's not restricted to men: the mother–daughter pair of Annette Karmiloff-Smith and Kyra Karmiloff (e.g. 2001) have collaborated to produce a masterly (if the term is not itself sexist) introduction to psycholinguistics. And it's not restricted to the western hemisphere or same-sex relationships: Ting-Chi Tang and Chih-Chen Jane

Tang, both known for their work on Chinese syntax (e.g. his 1992, her 2001), extend the range of the gene to East Asia and to male–female (father–daughter) relationships.

Of course, if linguistic ability is genetically determined it is not surprising that, as claimed in earlier unchallenged work (Smith, 1999), all linguists have other properties in common: specifically, that their names begin with a velar. Similarly, it is to be expected that possession of this gene entails that we have corresponding deficits elsewhere. For instance, Chomsky's being dialectically challenged may not be entirely idiosyncratic – maybe no linguist understands dialectics. It also follows that some poor people fail to be linguists only because they lack the relevant gene. These people should not be stigmatized for their defectiveness any more than those with heterosexual tendencies should be: it is simply beyond their control. Just as with sexual proclivities, one can of course struggle against one's genetic endowment in the linguistic domain: some people try to be linguists despite their genetic inadequacy. I leave it as an exercise for the reader to draw up lists of these benighted linguists manqués – their names will **not** begin with a velar.

Acknowledgements

A version of this chapter first appeared in 2003 in *Glot International* 7:202–3.

I am grateful to Janneke Balk for helpful discussions on genetics. She is not responsible for my continued obtuseness.

I am likewise grateful to Marit Westergaard for reminding me of the quotation from Roger Brown which forms the epigraph to this chapter.

Further reading

For a nice indication of the complexity of the effect of proteins, and a beautiful discussion of the genetics of human (ab)normality, see Leroi (2003); on talking to animals, see Anderson (2004).
Investigations of FOXP2 continue apace: see, for example, Corballis (2004).

11

Frogs, Parrots, Grooming, the Basal Ganglia and Language

. . . development . . . a partial fallacy
Encouraged by superficial notions of evolution.
T. S. Eliot, 'The Dry Salvages' (*Four Quartets*)

I once started a book by writing 'Frogs are not like us' (Smith, 2004:6). I had assumed that this was uncontroversial, but it seems I was wrong. Philip Lieberman (2001:21) has claimed that 'the neural basis of human language . . . crucially involves subcortical structures, the basal ganglia. The evolution of functional basal ganglia can be traced back in time to animals similar to present-day frogs . . . The evolution of human language, in this light, can be traced back hundreds of millions of years.' Well, yes. But maybe no: we rely for much of our metabolism on genetic specifications we share with mushrooms, but I doubt that even Lieberman would claim any relevant continuity between them and us (even if 'Bulgarian', for instance, can refer to either a fungus or a language).

Lieberman's striking assertion is the first shot in a sustained assault on many of the basic tenets of generative grammar. He argues against UG and its putative innateness, against the notion 'rule of grammar', and against the competence–performance distinction. He even denies the desirability of theoretical elegance in the evolutionary domain. Along the way he also argues against the existence of any neural architecture specific to language, against the localization of the language faculty, and hence against the possibility of deficits specific to language. His own position is encapsulated in the claim that 'language is not an instinct, based on genetically transmitted knowledge coded in a discrete cortical "language organ".

Instead it is a learned skill, based on a functional language system (FLS) that is distributed over many parts of the human brain' (2000:1). One final contentious claim among many is that speech is central and primary to language: sign is secondary.

These are all important issues and deserve careful dissection. Here I will just examine some of the more striking arguments and their putative implications. Ignoring for the moment the difference between Lieberman's 'FLS' and a Chomskyan 'Language Faculty', one can agree that 'subcortical structures are critical elements of the FLS that regulates human language and some aspects of cognition' (2001:37), but it's not obvious that any of Lieberman's more sensational conclusions follow from this. Most of the factual claims made are unexceptionable, but the consequences are not usually what is asserted. Consider, for instance, the observation that 'there is no evidence that the physiology of the brain differs in any fundamental manner for motor control and language' (2001:40); or that the importance of the basal ganglia is pervasive: thus, 'the "syntax" of rat grooming is regulated in the basal ganglia' (2001:25), and the 'basal ganglia circuitry implicated in motor control does not radically differ from that implicated in cognition' (2000:94; 2001:28).

The relevance of these claims to linguistics may seem marginal until we read (2000:158) that 'human language and thought can be regarded as neurally "computed" motor activity' (whatever that means); that the neural activity involved in the process of learning a language is 'similar to that by which a person learns to play a violin or a dog to retrieve balls' (2000:5); and that such 'biological facts all argue against neural structures that code innate linguistic knowledge such as the hypothetical "Universal Grammar" proposed by Noam Chomsky', where this UG and its associated 'rules' of syntax are anyway deemed to be 'biologically implausible' (2001:40).

The response to such reductionist assertions should be obvious: **linguistic** knowledge is made manifest in **psychological** processes which are carried out by **physiological** mechanisms instantiated in **physical** systems. But it doesn't follow that physiological generalizations can be stated in physical terms – for instance, in the vocabulary of particle physics – any more than it follows that psychological or linguistic generalizations can be stated in physiological terms – for example, in the vocabulary of neuro-anatomy. We need theories of each of these domains, and bridging statements connecting – hopefully unifying – the different theories. Ultimately we may be able to unify psychology and physiology by reducing one to the other, as physics and chemistry were unified in the last century; but that reduction only became possible after radical and unexpected changes to the physics (see Chomsky, 2000a:106f.), and we are still far from being able to effect any comparable unification relating knowledge of language to cortical or sub-cortical processes.

Clarifying the logic of Lieberman's attack leaves one in a better position to evaluate his other claims. It is fascinating to know that 'the proximate, opportunistic logic of evolution has produced a brain in which subcortical structures that regulate motor control in phylogenetically primitive animals are key components of circuits that regulate human language and thought' (2000:158–9), but nothing relevant to the putative innateness of (some aspects of) language follows from this. As Gallagher et al. (2002:155) spell out:

> the neurological processes that underlie speech, hand gestures, facial expressions, the perception of action, imitation, social cognition and interaction might share some common pathways, especially at their 'lower' levels, with the computational processes that underlie locomotive or instrumental movement. But they also involve brain processes independent of areas concerned with purely instrumental movement and so are not reducible simply to motor processes.

As part of his campaign, Lieberman is at pains to defend a distributed model of the FLS, contrasting his position with Chomsky's modular view that 'the human brain contains a unique **localized** "language organ" ' (Lieberman 2000:8; my emphasis). If knowledge of language is 'distributed', rather than strictly localized, would this undermine the generative view of the language faculty? Chomsky's own position is more nuanced than one might infer from the characterization in this quotation. Consider the following passage from the paper Lieberman was referring to:

> The question of localization of language function is one on which I am not competent to comment . . . But even if it were to turn out that there are no specific areas of the brain in which language function is localized, still there are surely specific mechanisms involved in the representation of language knowledge and the capacity to use this knowledge . . . Hence the question of localization, while an

interesting one, does not seem to me to have overriding importance.
(Chomsky 1980:49)

Lieberman's preconceptions about localization are not unusual;
his views on the nature of science more generally are off the wall.
He asserts, entirely correctly, that scientific theories must be tested,
but the main criterion he suggests is bizarre: 'theoretical linguists
must take into account the degree to which a particular theory
describes the sentences of a corpus' (2000:165–6), whereas elegance
and simplicity are irrelevant, because 'evolution is a tinkerer'.
More specifically, 'there is no logical reason why neural structures
that control locomotion in human beings also play a part in
thinking. Evolution does not give a damn about formal elegance'
(2000:166). But scientific theories do not 'evolve' in the way that
organic systems do, and the repeated success of a strategy emphasizing the elegance of theories in the biological domain as in the
physical domain is unlikely to be just a coincidence. The implied
need for concentration on a corpus is likewise unmotivated.
Corpora may be valuable tools, but they rarely exhibit the range
of possibilities – still less the impossibilities – that are characteristic of our knowledge of language.

A similar mix of mystification and over-simplification becomes
apparent in another plank in Lieberman's argumentation: his
claim that 'speech is a central, if not the central, feature of human
linguistic ability' (2000:157). The importance of this tenet is seen
in his exaggerated claims for the linguistic abilities of other species.
'Syntactic ability, which generally is taken by linguists . . . to be a
unique human attribute, is present to a limited degree in language-
trained chimpanzees . . . The sole aspect of human linguistic ability
that chimpanzees lack is speech' (2001:37). Leaving aside the
remarkable transition from 'a limited degree' to 'the **sole** aspect',
this claim is contentious for other reasons. Laura-Ann Petitto has
argued repeatedly (e.g. Petitto, 1999:48) that 'the genetic foundations of language are not at the level of modality [speech versus
sign] but at the level of abstract features of language structure'.
That is, speech is merely the most common surface manifestation
of an abstract linguistic ability which can surface equally well in
signed mode.

Evidence against this claim, hence indirectly in favour of
Lieberman's position, might be gleaned from the fact that deaf

children indulge in vocal babbling at the same age as hearing children. This seems to indicate a priority for spoken language, but Petitto et al. (2001) have recently shown that even hearing babies, who have been exposed to sign rather than spoken language by their deaf parents, babble manually rather than vocally. Interestingly, their manual babbling displays the same rhythms as occur in spoken language. Modality neutrality rather than priority for speech seems to be the most plausible explanation for this parallelism.

Perhaps one could find evidence in favour of Lieberman's position in Pepperberg's work on parrots, which are phylogenetically rather distant from humans (and frogs). Apparently (Pepperberg, 2002:154), parrots not only come up with novel utterances like *wanna green nut* and *do you want grape?* but show 'simultaneous emergence of both vocal and physical combinatorial behaviour', so 'the neural machinery involved in making ordered word and object patterns is not unique to primates'. Fascinating. But again the implications for the nature of the human language faculty, either ontogenetic or phylogenetic, seem to be minimal.

There is a variety of other misrepresentations and unsubstantiated innuendoes in Lieberman's work. First, he repeats the usual canard that Chomsky denies that language evolved (2000:15; 127f.; see Jenkins, 2000, and Smith, 2002:ch. 15, for discussion). Second, Lieberman inconsistently uses changes in the theory to argue that 'the competence/performance distinction is often used to reject data that falsify the current theory' (2000:14), making it 'impossible to test theory against data' (p. 13). This is part of a more general claim that 'the competence/performance distinction is biologically implausible' (p. 15). Third, he says that 'deficits limited to specific fragments of grammar have never been documented' (2000:165). There is, of course, no reference to prime examples of such documentation as van der Lely's (1998) discussion of Specific Language Impairment (SLI) or Davies's (2002) theoretical account of the condition. Lieberman does refer to the KE family, saying only that 'their behavioral [sic] deficits in all likelihood derive from impairment of the striatal components of the functional language system' (2000:129–30). They may indeed, but how this would account for the details of the linguistic problems they have, or for the existence of SLI more generally, remains obscure.

Continuing to dissect this rather distasteful book might be cathartic, but enough is enough. Lieberman makes great play with the notion 'biological plausibility', yet using his criteria, humans in general turn out to be pretty implausible, and their linguistic abilities even less likely. However, there are lots of us around and I still don't think frogs are like us.

Acknowledgement

This chapter first appeared in 2002 in *Glot International* 6:168–70.

Further reading

For recent discussion of innateness, see, for instance, chapter 8 above, and Samuels (2004).

For discussion of the evolution of language, see Hauser et al. (2002). A useful overview of the issues appears in Christiansen and Kirby (2003); see also Nowak and Komarova (2001) and the papers in Briscoe (2002).

Part III

Core Concerns

12

Parametric Poverty

. . . too little is understood to venture any strong hypotheses.
Noam Chomsky, *The Minimalist Program*,
discussing parametric variation

Word learning is easy. From the age of two to twelve children learn around one new word every waking hour of their lives, with the implication that many of these words are learnt on the basis of rather minimal exposure (Bloom, 2000:25). Learning the properties of words is also the main basis for the acquisition of syntax, with the range of parametric variation restricted (perhaps) to the formal features of functional categories. But the notion of learning in the two domains is different. In learning the relationship between a particular sound and meaning – that [peŋgwin] picks out particular sphenisciform birds, for instance – the child typically receives obvious, robust evidence. In learning the selectional properties of a complementizer, or the possibility of parasitic gaps, the task is not so straightforward, and we are confronted with Plato's problem: how we can end up knowing so much when the evidence is so meagre.

The solution to this problem of the poverty of the stimulus is supposed to lie in parameter fixing. Exposure to particular data triggers the child to acquire knowledge that goes beyond those data, and Plato's problem dissolves. Although 'one-off learning' may be enough to fix the relation between a sound and a meaning (complex though even this is), it is implausible that it could work for the acquisition of syntax. You probably need to hear more than one example of *tough*-movement to decide that you are indeed acquiring English rather than languages like Finnish or Tsez which don't have it (p.c. from respectively Anders Holmberg and Maria Polinsky). Moreover, children are notoriously more resistant to correction in the syntactic domain than in the lexical domain. Martin Braine's (1971) famous example of his daughter's persistence, despite repeated correction, in saying 'other one spoon' is in stark contrast with the absence of such examples for simple lexical learning. We simply do not find exchanges of the non-existent, and indeed impossible, kind:

> *Child*:   Whose cat is that?
> *Adult*:   That's not a cat, it's a hamster.
> *Child*:   But whose cat is it?

This impossible dialogue suggests that the two learning processes are rather different, and that for syntax there may be a frequency threshold which has to be crossed before learning is assured.

So what happens in the face of such 'parametric poverty', when the data are too sparse to have a triggering function? There seem to be three possibilities: default settings, random settings and no settings, each of which has some plausibility. Evidence for the possibility of 'default settings' for particular parametric choices comes from the existence of language acquisition data where minimal input seems to lead to the same result across children and languages. *Pro*-drop is the obvious candidate. Nina Hyams (1986) once argued for the claim that the *pro*-drop parameter has a default positive setting [+*pro*-drop], thereby accounting for the apparent absence of parametric differences in the output of children learning *pro*-drop and non-*pro*-drop languages. Appealing though this idea is, there turned out to be serious empirical and theoretical problems with the notion 'default'. The empirical problem was that the null subjects characteristic of children's speech had quite different properties from the null subjects of *pro*-drop languages, entailing that a default value of the adult parameter was not the way to view the acquisition data. The theoretical problem was that the notion 'default' turned out to be arbitrary, with some parameters having a default value and others not; with the result that a principled characterization of the notion proved impossible (Borer and Wexler, 1987). In consequence, defaults – at least in this area – have been largely abandoned.

The second possibility is that there are 'random settings'. Given the same input, different children might assign the same parameter different values. Support for such a possibility comes from the existence in the adult language of dialectal and idiolectal differences, where the speakers are in other respects similar, perhaps even members of the same family. It is well known that different people allow different sequence of tense possibilities (see chapter 7 above). For many speakers *Did you know that Emily is ill?* is simply ungrammatical, and only *Did you know that Emily was ill?* is possible; for me both are fine, though the former has a marked interpretation in which the speaker takes some responsibility for the truth of the embedded proposition. Here we have a situation in which intuitions are completely clear cut, so the relevant parameter has been fixed, but it has been fixed apparently at random, presumably because of the paucity of distinguishing data.

The phenomenon is widespread and even generalizes to phonology: Moira Yip (2003:804) gives an example where evidence from language games suggests that some people treat a postconsonantal glide as a secondary articulation of the consonant, others as a segment in its own right: 'the rightful home of /y/ [is] underdetermined by the usual data, leaving room for variation'. Her conclusion is that 'speakers opt for different structures in the absence of conclusive evidence for either'.

A more complex example is provided by differences in *that*-trace effects. The usual paradigm, exemplified by the contrast between *Who do you think left?* and **Who do you think that left?*, conceals a multitude of variation. As Cowart (1997) demonstrates, many informants are wildly inconsistent in their judgements of such sentences, even though 'highly stable patterns may be discernible in data from a group of informants without those same patterns being readily detectable in the results of individual informants' (1997:35). This suggests the third, less orthodox, 'no setting' scenario.

The idea that children's categories are unset or under-specified *vis-à-vis* their adult congeners is common enough as a temporary stage in the process of first language acquisition: the parameter is simply unfixed. A nice example is provided by Anderson's interesting (2002) discussion of *tough*-movement. She reports that children characteristically go through an 'intermediate' stage in the acquisition of *tough*-movement constructions, in which they accept and produce both adult-like and non-adult-like interpretations for sentences such as *The frog is hard to ride*. For these children the sentence can mean either that it is hard (for the hedgehog) to ride the frog, or that it is hard for the frog to ride (the hedgehog). No current adult variety of English is like this, so the co-existence of two interpretive options differentiates the child grammar from the adult one in a striking way. The simplest explanation is that the relevant parameter, associated with a small set of lexical items, has simply not (yet) been set, leaving both subject and object options open.

Such under-specification is supposedly characteristic only of child grammars (Hyams, 1996:105); and in the adult grammar the relevant details of the previously under-specified form will be filled in. But suppose that this never happens, and we end up with some parameters still indeterminate in the adult language. What might constitute evidence for this superficially unlikely situation? The existence of 'delicate judgements' where you may simply not be sure of your own intuitions seems to support such a possibility.

As we saw above, *that*-trace phenomena indicate that there is more than one dialect around: for instance, Cowart reports (1997:82) that of seventy-one informants whom he tested 'about one in ten showed a reversal of the standard *that*-trace pattern'. Given the paucity of the input data, such variation may be expected, suggesting that different populations have set the relevant parameter(s) differently. What is less expected is the amount of variation in particular individuals, who show inconsistent and labile intuitions. In the *that*-trace examples, the same informants often gave different judgements for the same sentence on different occasions, or different judgements for two sentences illustrating the same construction on the same occasion. One explanation of such indeterminacy is that the relevant parameter remains unspecified for these speakers.

A natural reaction to the suggestion that there may be unset parameters is to argue that they really have been set, but that complexities of processing and pragmatic considerations conspire to make one accept examples outside one's real grammar. It is undoubtedly true that the longer and more complex a sentence, the easier it is to persuade oneself that it is not really as bad as its shorter and simpler congener; but this is probably not pertinent to the tests used by Cowart. Alternatively, it might be suggested that fluctuating judgements can arise if a speaker is bi-dialectal, using varieties with opposite parameter settings. A dialect switch during a test could then be caused by local interference, such as the presence of particular words in the example, or by the sociolinguistic accommodation (in the sense of Giles et al., 1991) which pushes speakers to modulate their production to that of their interlocutors. The freedom with which individuals in bilingual communities indulge in code switching supports this last possibility.

There is almost certainly an element of truth in each of these suggestions, but they are nonetheless insufficient to account for the complex nature of our intuitions. Everyone is familiar with the experience of just not being sure what their judgement of a particular example is, and any such instance is a candidate for an explanation appealing to an unset parameter. Moreover, there seems to be a systematic difference between examples where we know from repeated exposure that some people use X to mean Y even though we cannot, and genuine insecurity in being able to tell whether we can or cannot say X at all. A simple example of the former is provided by any kind of recognized dialect alternation. In many (mainly American) varieties of English, it is customary to say *We didn't see him yet*, which for me, despite long-standing familiarity, is simply ungrammatical (I have to use the alternative *We haven't seen him yet*). An example of the latter (for me) comes from the scope of negation in examples like *All the children aren't coming*, when used to mean *None of the children is coming*. After meditating on the matter for forty years or so, I am no longer quite as certain as I used to be that the reading is impossible. Crucially, there is a clear distinction between having no judgement – where one is simply not sure what the 'facts' are – and vacillating between two judgements like a gestalt switch.

It is not only processing considerations that affect one's intuitions: pragmatic considerations may likewise intervene. The example *Did you know that Emily was ill?* is ambiguous between interpretations where the illness is current, with the tense linked to speech time, and past, where it is linked to reference time. The version that 'violates' the sequence of tense rule, *Did you know that Emily is ill?*, is not only pragmatically restricted to situations where the speaker endorses the fact of the illness, it is also unambiguously present tense. The advantage of such disambiguation may be a factor in persuading some speakers, whose grammar strictly disallows it, to find it nonetheless acceptable in parsing and production.

All these considerations may play a role, but I still think they leave the option of having unset parameters viable. The question remains why the possibility of both random settings and no settings should co-exist. It may be that there is no setting until one is forced in production to make a (random) choice – a choice one can usually avoid. More research is needed: only a closer analysis of inter- and intra-idiolectal variation will reveal the true limits to parameter setting.

Acknowledgement

This chapter was written jointly with Annabel Cormack, and first appeared in 2002 in *Glot International* 6:285–7. She has recently extended the argument in a paper with Ian Roberts (Cormack and Roberts, 2004).

Further reading

For a clear introduction to the theory of parameters, see Baker (2001b, 2003). For interesting discussion of (differential) optionality in child and adult language, see van Kampen (2004). For recent discussion of differences between null subjects in adult and child language, see Rizzi (2002).

13

Linguistics by Numbers

Numerical precision is the very soul of science.
D'Arcy Thompson, *On Growth and Form*

I once wrote a disparaging article (Smith, 1989a:ch. 16) about the misuse of quantitative techniques in linguistics, and argued that 'in general the numbers game is irrelevant to the [theoretical] linguist'. I then proceeded to pour scorn on a variety of silly examples in the literature where sundry scholars had taken to counting things (apparently, because that seemed to be easier than actually thinking). Times change. I still think the victims of my earlier scorn deserved it, but it is no longer intellectually defensible for even the most theoretically oriented linguist to dismiss statistical analysis the way I did. Moreover, the results of such analysis may have interesting implications for core notions of current theory.

Consider to begin with an example from first language acquisition. Children and adults typically give different interpretations to sentences containing universal quantifiers. For instance, given a situation in which three penguins are holding a fish each, children and adults alike assent to the proposition that 'Every penguin is holding a fish.' However, if you add another fish, unattached to any penguin, and ask 'Is every penguin holding a fish?', adults still reply 'Yes', whereas children systematically say 'No', often with a spontaneous elaboration of the kind 'This fish is all alone.' This phenomenon of 'quantifier spreading' is well known and has been widely discussed for half a century or so. But to decide which quantifiers spread, whether they spread from left to right or right to left (or both), whether bare plurals behave the same way as overtly quantified NPs, what role is played by the syntactic contexts they spread in, at what ages children attain adult-like competence, whether the phenomenon is universal or learners of different languages differ in their progress, whether the correct explanation is to be attributed to development in the grammar or in cognition – all this requires group studies using large numbers of children, backed up by detailed statistical analysis. In a recent book (Kang, 2002), Hye-Kyung Kang provides tentative answers to many of these questions. She argues on the basis of her statistically analysed experiments in Korean and English that the phenomenon is general, perhaps universal, and that children's differential sensitivity to syntactic configuration – including island effects – demonstrates that the aetiology of the spreading is linguistic. Interestingly, she also argues that the different error rates found in the performance of different age groups suggest that a cognitive component is involved in the progression, and she makes explicit suggestions about the interaction of the central system and the language faculty in this domain. All this is good 'normal science' in Kuhn's (1970) sense, but none of it would have been possible without quantitative data.

Let us turn from language acquisition to language change. For the last twenty years or so, Tony Kroch and his colleagues (see e.g. Kroch, 1989, 2002; Haeberli, 2002; Pintzuk, 2002; etc.) have been using regression analysis to illuminate historical syntax. Among other insights, he has demonstrated that it is possible to give an account of syntactic drift which can accommodate its gradual, incremental character within a generative framework which treats syntactic change as abrupt grammatical reorganization. For instance, if one looks at the history of periphrastic *do* in English, it is clear that its development extends over several centuries with significant differences in its incidence in different linguistic environments: declaratives, negatives, questions, negative questions, and so on. Kroch argues that the spread of *do* is a unitary phenomenon that should be analysed as 'a gradual change in the relative frequencies of competing forms' (1989:138), where the competition is a function of processing complexity. More particularly, he also argues that the grammar has a crucial 'mediating' influence, constraining the effect on frequencies of this processing complexity. In the present context this predicts that 'the rate of increase in the use of *do* should be the same in all environments' (1989:155) – a surprising conclusion given that the psycholinguistic motivation for the increase

is different in each case, and sometimes even non-existent. His conclusion has since been substantiated in a number of other domains,
including verb-second effects and the loss of OV word order, the
position of negation, and the placing of adjuncts. In every case the
results are dependent on the use of sophisticated statistical techniques: without a mathematical model there is simply no way of
deciding among competing hypotheses.

A further advantage of such quantitative analyses is that they
dissolve the tension faced by historical linguists between I-language
and E-language. That is, the frequent perception that historical
syntax is unamenable to theoretical treatment, because it deals with
random exemplars of E-language rather than with the products of
the mentally represented I-language, is misconceived. An E-language
change may be instantiated over several centuries, but the rules
of the grammar (the I-language) which is reorganized (once one
form has been entirely displaced by its competitors) have the same
psychological status as in any synchronic account of competence.

This consideration of I-language leads on to another intriguing
use of statistics: the attempt by Wayne Cowart (e.g. 1997) to make
intuitions respectable. The use of native speaker judgements, or
intuitions, has been a central and extremely fruitful feature of
generative grammar for half a century. But it's no use basing an
argument on intuitional judgements if no one else shares them.
I'm constantly irritated by having to construct my own examples
which **are** grammatical, because the original author has provided
only suspect examples. Quite often it doesn't matter, as finding an
alternative 'good' example is merely the work of a few minutes.
For instance, two of my colleagues – Misi Brody and Rita Manzini
(1988) – once began a paper on implicit arguments with the
example 'Mary was saying to leave.' For me this sentence is simply unacceptable and, I assume, ungrammatical. Fortunately, they
provided enough examples with which I did agree to assuage my
scepticism about the validity of the theoretical arguments based on
them. But it shouldn't be the reader who has to do such work,
especially as the reader can't do such work if he or she is not a
native speaker. Clearly, one has to take examples from languages
and dialects with which one is not familiar on trust, but when one
thinks one speaks the same language as the author, and one dis-
agrees with **all** the relevant examples, doubts about the validity of
the argument being constructed become persistent. Consider in this

respect Idan Landau's (2000) book on control. A substantial part of this is dedicated to arguing for a notion of 'partial control', exemplified by instances such as (1), which is supposed to contrast with the ungrammatical (2):

1.   Mary wondered whether [PRO to apply together for the grant]
2.   *Mary applied together for the grant

Landau writes that sentences like (1) 'require some contextual setting . . . [which] can be easily constructed' (Landau, 2000:27). But whatever the setting, for me (1) is just as bad as (2). In fact, all the relevant examples he provides are unacceptable to me and to all those I have (unsystematically) consulted. This is unfortunate, as the putative contrast has 'dramatic consequences for the proper semantic treatment of control' (Landau, 2000:29). There are, presumably, rather different implications if there is no contrast in grammaticality. If the data had come from Hebrew or Hindi, I should simply have accepted them, albeit with mild surprise. Maybe, in fact, they do come from another language. As there is no linguistic difference between a language and a dialect, it would not be too surprising to find that other varieties of English allowed the examples I find unacceptable. But then it is crucial that we be told which variety of English this is, and how dependable the status of the intuitive judgements is. If we don't have such information, future researchers may fall into the trap of assuming that these 'facts' are true of all varieties, with potentially unfortunate consequences. It is fairly clear that the union of the two systems (Landau's and mine) is not the product of a consistent grammar, hence not one which characterizes a possible human language. Defining possible human languages is presumably one of our basic aims as linguists.

It gets worse. As Cowart (1997) demonstrates, many informants are wildly inconsistent in their judgements of example sentences. Discussing *that*-trace effects, he makes the striking observation that 'highly stable patterns may be discernible in data from a group of informants without those same patterns being readily detectable in the results of individual informants' (1997:35). Previously (see chapter 12 above) Annabel Cormack and I used this fact to support a heterodox view of parameter setting; but taken at face value it also seems to have implications for the validity of restricting the domain of theoretical inquiry to I-language. If it is true that the generalizations we want to attribute to I-language sometimes only become apparent on the basis of group data and are not apparent in the judgements of any individual, does this undermine the 'individual', 'internal', 'intensional' basis of current theory? Cowart is at pains to emphasize that no such conclusion would be warranted: the use of group data enables us to come up with results that are statistically reliable for the population as a whole. In principle, we could amass sufficient data for any one individual by testing and retesting him or her fifty times for each sentence. It's just that most of the colleagues and students we rely on for informant judgements are not patient enough to make that feasible.

The kind of work done by Cowart, and others such as Carson Schütze (1996), can provide a solid quantitative basis for the claims practising syntacticians make. Psychologists have always used quantitative data. We should give up our statistical scepticism, take a leaf out of their book and learn to count.

Acknowledgements

This chapter originally appeared in 2003 in *Glot International* 7:110–12.

A more accessible summary of Hye-Kyung Kang's results appears in her (2001).

Postscript

Idan Landau assures me that all the judgements he reports were widely tested on a number of speakers of American English. I have since tried the examples on speakers of American English and found that some of them do, and some of them do not, share Landau's intuitions. So the data do 'come from another language'.

14

Modules, Modals, Maths and the Mind

Every thinking human . . . is a numerical being.
Richard Dedekind, cited in Heike Wiese,
Numbers, Language and the Human Mind

The standard cliché has it that the human mind/brain is the most complex entity in the universe. Understanding such complexity requires the genius of simplification, and no one has been better at this than Jerry Fodor. He has been responsible for two of the most controversial, and fruitful, claims in the psychology of mind and language. In his 1975 book, *The Language of Thought*, he argued that you cannot learn a language with greater expressive power than one you already know, hence that there must be a rich innate language of thought. In his 1983 classic, *The Modularity of Mind*, while arguing that the structure of the mind is in part modular, he suggested that the 'central system', responsible for puzzle solving and the fixation of belief, was both non-modular and pretty much inscrutable. Though there have been significant changes in his thinking over the last twenty to thirty years, these still seem to reflect his basic beliefs. But recent research indicates that both positions may be wrong.

Let's start with modularity. I wish to impugn only one half of Fodor's claim about the modularity of mind: I am still convinced of the validity of his characterization of 'input systems' such as vision and audition in terms of their being domain-specific, fast, mandatory, informationally encapsulated, and so on. But the structure of the central system seems to be less opaque than his pessimistic observations suggest. Of the proposals around, many owe their inspiration ultimately to Chomsky's (1975, 1984) notion of module. For current purposes I shall use the framework that Ianthi Tsimpli and I have been developing over a number of years, exploiting the idea that the central system is compartmentalized into a number of **quasi-modules** (Smith, 2003a; Tsimpli and Smith, 1998). Quasi-modules are like Fodorian modules, but use a conceptual (not a perceptual) vocabulary, and are not informationally encapsulated: that is, they can 'talk' to each other. Examples are Theory of Mind, Moral Judgement, Music, Common Sense, Social structure, the Number Sense, Personality structure, Folk Physics, Folk Biology, and more. The full set of such faculties is a matter of ongoing debate, but reasonably clear evidence for at least this inventory comes from the existence of 'double dissociations', where different subjects may lose one ability while retaining another and vice versa (Smith, 1998b). Language is a special case: it seems to be partly modular in Fodor's sense, and partly quasi-modular (Smith and Tsimpli, 1995). The details are complex, and there is also the need to accommodate the emotions (see chapter 18 below), but this is enough to be getting on with. Looking at the interrelations among Language, Theory of Mind (ToM), and Number will cast light on the claims I started with.

The evidence comes from the growth of the child's linguistic abilities and how these feed into and are influenced by the development of other modules of the mind, especially Theory of Mind and the Number sense. 'Theory of Mind' is the mental faculty that enables us to adopt the viewpoint of other people, even where this leads to our entertaining representations of the world that differ from our own or from the 'truth'. I may be convinced that the prime minister is a war criminal, but nevertheless know that you consider him a paragon of every virtue. Such conflicting views do not lead to contradiction, precisely because I can attribute them 'meta-representationally' to different people. This ability is not present in two-year-old children, but develops gradually around the ages of three to four, as manifest in the ability to pass so-called false belief tasks such as 'Sally-Anne' and 'Smarties' (see e.g. Wellman, 1990). For current purposes what is relevant is the role of meta-representation in the child's developing mastery of modal verbs like *must*.

There is an (apparent) ambiguity between 'deontic' (or 'root') and 'epistemic' uses of modals (plus a possible third 'alethic' interpretation (Smith, 1989b)), as shown in the three versions of (1) given in (2):

1.   You must be unmarried

2a.   [To enter this competition] you must be
     unmarried   {deontic/root}
  b.   [To go out as much as you do] you must
      be unmarried   {epistemic}
  c.   [To be a bachelor] you must be unmarried   {alethic}

It has been known for some time that in first language acquisition root meanings appear consistently earlier than epistemic ones (see e.g. Sweetser, 1990:50). Why should this be? In insightful work, Anna Papafragou (1998) has suggested an explanation: appropriate use of epistemic modality presupposes the emergence of the meta-representational ability characteristic of Theory of Mind. It is only when the proprietary vocabulary of this module of the mind has emerged that the language faculty develops the (meta-) representational ability to handle the extra complexity of epistemic interpretation.

The developmental relationship between language and Theory of Mind is actually bi-directional. There is independent evidence that 'language acquisition . . . is causally necessary for the development of ToM' (Garfield et al., 2001:520); in particular, the development of '*that*-clauses' is necessary for the emergence of Theory of Mind (de Villiers and de Villiers, 2000; see also Papafragou, 2002). The representational expressive power of language underpins the emergence of Theory of Mind; the meta-representational expressive power of Theory of Mind underpins a specific linguistic ability. In the normally developing individual there is constant interaction between the developing quasi-modules: they develop side by side, with each one feeding into the other at crucial developmental stages. In some (autistic) people, by contrast, Theory of Mind fails to develop fully, even though their knowledge of language may in other respects be intact. The reverse dissociation may occur in Down syndrome children, whose Theory of Mind may function normally, but whose language may be impaired. That is, despite the normal interactions, the double dissociation indicates the potential autonomy of the two faculties.

This interdependence suggests that, in the domain of language, informational encapsulation is not absolute, and that Fodor's pessimistic view of the central system needs revision. Even if this is correct, it leaves unimpugned the more radical, and earlier, claim that you cannot acquire a representational system of greater expressive power than one you already possess. But elegant research on the interaction of the Number Sense (Dehaene, 1997) and the Language Faculty by Elizabeth Spelke and Sanna Tsivkin suggests that even this needs some hedging. One strand of their work suggests that language is 'a medium for conceptual change' (Spelke and Tsivkin, 2001:71; see also Feigenson et al., 2004), and that this change can lead to an 'enrichment' of the whole system, implying that Fodor's claim that it is impossible to learn a language of greater expressive power than one you already have may need revising.

Our knowledge of number is not unitary, but consists of three sub-parts. First, without needing to count, we are able to perceive the exact number of items presented to us: we can 'subitize' 1, 2, 3 and perhaps 4, but nothing larger. That is, when shown three penguins or two owls, or (perhaps) four sheep, we can say instantly how many penguins, owls or sheep there are, but we are unable to do this with larger numbers. This 'capacity for representing the exact numerosity of small sets is common to humans and other animals and emerges early [i.e. pre-linguistically] in human development' (Spelke and Tsivkin, 2001:82–3). Second, and still without counting, we can entertain 'approximate' representations of sets of all sizes, such as the difference between displays of eight versus sixteen items (but not that between six versus eight, which are too close). This ability too emerges in infancy and is shared with other animals. It persists into adulthood in the ability to give estimates such as 'about twenty'. In principle, either of these systems can be used in the identification of small sets. Finally, human **adults** – but not infants and animals – have a third system: verbal counting using the natural numbers. 1, 2, 3 . . . 7, 8, 9 . . . *ad infinitum*.

The core of Spelke and Tsivkin's claim is then that: 'Children may attain the mature system of knowledge of the natural numbers by conjoining together the representations delivered by their two preverbal systems. Language may serve as a medium for this conjunction, . . . because it is a domain-general, combinatorial system to which the representations delivered by the child's two non-verbal systems can be mapped' (Spelke and Tsivkin, 2001:84).

Consider the number 'two'. This can be represented by the young child either by exploiting subitizing: 'an object x and an object y' (where x and y are distinct), or by exploiting approximation: described as 'a blur on the number line indicating a very small set' (Spelke and Tsivkin, 2001:85; citing Gelman and Gallistel, 1978). Once language develops, the child observes syntactic consistency: numbers are used for subitizing and for approximating, and occur systematically in the same syntactic configurations. This leads it to attempt to fuse the two systems. For instance, it knows that 'two' is used to refer to particular small sets Then, given 'seven', for which **neither** of its systems is adequate, it may (gradually) infer – from its knowledge of '1, 2, 3', together with the observation that they are part of a counting sequence which includes '7' – that 'seven' also refers to sets of objects with comparable sequential properties. This new system that the child has developed is then intrinsically more powerful than either of the pre-linguistic systems it started with and, perhaps, more powerful than the language on which the development is parasitic.

Corroborative evidence for this argument comes from dissociations in pathology (Dehaene, 1997) and experiments on bilinguals. Patients with different kinds of cerebral lesion doubly dissociate with regard to their ability to cope with small (subitized) numbers and approximations on the one hand, and with exact large numbers on the other, where this latter difficulty typically correlates with a language deficit. Such **dis**sociations suggest that the different parts of the number system are stored differently in the brain, and the **as**sociation suggests that only the exact manipulation of large numbers is dependent on the language faculty. This language dependence is borne out by bilingual studies: when Russian–English bilinguals performed calculations requiring rough estimates of cube roots, they showed no dependence on the language used; when they performed operations requiring exact, large-number calculations, these appeared to be processed in a language-specific form (Spelke and Tsivkin, 2001:88f).

The elegant simplicity of Fodor's ideas has not been overthrown: the interpretations summarized here are far from demonstrative; but the issues he has raised are firmly back on the research agenda. Even his apparently *a priori* argument turns out to be empirical.

Acknowledgement

A version of this chapter first appeared in 2002 in *Glot International* 6:248–50.

Further reading

For discussion of the interaction of the development of language and cognition, see Clark (2004); for recent work on bilingualism, see French and Jacquet (2004); on double dissociation, see now Caramazza and Shapiro (2004).

For a recent survey of work in Theory of Mind, see Leslie et al. (2004). The basic claims about Theory of Mind and its emergence have recently been cast into doubt in work by Onishi and Baillargeon (submitted).

15

Nothing

Naturall reason abhorreth vacuum.

Thomas Cranmer, *Lord's Supper*

Academic specialization results in people knowing more and more about less and less until they know everything about nothing. I still don't know everything, but I've have been an academic linguist long enough to give me an excuse to write about nothing: about 'zero', or 'empty categories' as we tend to put it.

The use of zero in linguistic description has been around since Panini's Astadhyayi, the amazing grammar of Sanskrit produced in about 500 BC, shortly after Indian mathematicians had invented zero[1] in a different domain. One might think that such a pedigree would guarantee acceptance of the concept, but while everyone agrees that zero is ineliminable in mathematics, there has been repeated resistance to accepting it in the description of language.

The most basic use of zero involves examples as simple as *cats* and *sheep*. The singular–plural relation between *cat* and *cats* is manifestly the same as that between *sheep* and *sheep*, but in the former the plural is marked by the addition of the suffix -*s*, whereas in the latter it is marked by nothing. The conclusion is obvious: the form of the plural may in some cases be zero, from which it is but a short step to the claim that there is actually an element present in such examples. It is not that there is nothing there, but rather that what is there has no visible or audible substance. A comparable claim is made for the article, with one of the standard reference works (Greenbaum and Quirk, 1990:71) arguing that: 'The absence of article in *I like Freda* and *I like music* makes the two nouns only superficially similar; in the former there is *no article* where in the latter there is *zero article* which can contrast with *the*.' Before deciding whether this subtle distinction is well motivated, let's look at a wider range of examples of empty categories. I'll list half a dozen.

First, there is the kind of 'understood subject' familiar from traditional grammar and illustrated in (1), where the crossed-out element may or may not be pronounced, but is understood as being syntactically and semantically present. This is obvious in that *go home* is interpreted as being addressed to '*you*' whether '*you*' is mentioned or not:

1. ~~you~~ *go home*

Second, we have an extension of the same phenomenon with what is known as 'PRO', the invisible subject of a non-finite clause, illustrated in (2b). The usual analysis rests on the assumption that the structure of the two examples in (2) is the same: in each case John wants something, and what he wants is that someone go – either *you* or himself. That is, the verb *go* always has a subject, whether overt or covert – 'empty', in other words:

2a. John wants [you to go]
 b. John$_i$ wants [PRO$_i$ to go]

The subscript simply makes explicit that the subject of *go* is the same person, *John*, as is the subject of *wants*.

Third, we have other kinds of ellipsed material: empty verbs as in the 'gapped' example in (3), empty auxiliaries as in (4), empty complementizers as in (5), and so on:

3. John ate a halibut and Mary ~~ate~~ a hake

4. John might eat a sandwich and Mary ~~might~~ drink a beer

5. I think ~~that~~ penguins taste delicious

There is an obvious principle of least effort at work in these cases: repeating the same verb or auxiliary in adjacent clauses is a waste of energy, and as the hearer can be expected to have no difficulty in working out what the speaker intends to communicate it is simplest just to leave them out.

Determiners may also be empty; you can say either that *polar bears hibernate in the winter* or that *polar bears hibernate in winter*: the presence of *the* seems to make no difference (see the next chapter, '*The*', for more complex examples). This potential emptiness becomes particularly clear when you compare English with other languages. English and French differ systematically, as shown by (6):

6a.   I'm studying Danish
 b.   J'étudie le danois

The examples in (6) have identical semantic interpretation, but the presence of the article (*le*) is obligatory in French and impossible in English: *I'm studying the Danish* and *J'étudie danois* are both ungrammatical. This interpretive identity suggests that there is some level of representation at which the two sentences have the same structure, but if this is the case then it becomes plausible to assume that there is an empty determiner in English parallel to the visible one in French. There is in fact corroborative evidence for such an assumption in selectional facts. Different elements 'select' particular items with which they can co-occur: *deride* selects a following object, but *snigger* has no such selectional possibility (though it can be followed by a Prepositional Phrase), with the result that the examples in (7) are acceptable, but those in (8) are ungrammatical:

7a.   She derided my efforts
 b.   She sniggered (at my efforts)

8a.   *She derided (at my efforts)
 b.   *She sniggered my efforts

As Radford (2004a:115) points out, the empty determiner has not only the property of being invisible, but it too has selectional properties, as illustrated by the examples in (9), which show that the null determiner has the same privilege of occurrence as the overt item *enough*:

9a. I write poems/poetry/*poem
  b. I've written enough poems/poetry/*poem

Selectional properties are specified in the lexical entry of each item, but that entails that such items **have** a lexical entry – they exist, even if they are invisible.

Fourth, there are various 'traces' marking the movement of constituents that have been displaced from their usual position: for example, NP or WH – that is, a phrase containing a Wh-word such as *what* or *which* – as in (10):

10a. What$_i$ did John put t$_i$ in the wheelbarrow?
  b. [His grandson]$_i$, John put t$_i$ in the wheelbarrow[2]

One of the properties of *put* is that it must normally be followed by both a NP and a Prepositional Phrase (PP), so that the omission of either results in ungrammaticality, as shown in (11):

11a. John put his grandson in the wheelbarrow
  b. *John put in the wheelbarrow
  c. *John put his grandson

(10a) contains the overt sequence *John put in the wheelbarrow* that (11b) shows is ungrammatical, yet (10a) is fine. There are various ways of accounting for such patterns, but the standard one is to assume that *what* in (10a) and *his grandson* in (10b) originate in the position of the trace (t$_i$), as in the 'echo-question' *John put what in the wheelbarrow?*, and it is this trace of movement that satisfies the requirement of *put* to have a following NP. Again, the logic of the argument is that such things as traces must be present even if you can't see (or hear) them.

But sometimes you can hear them. Empty categories are defined as elements which are phonologically empty: they are not pronounced, but which have syntactic and semantic effects. In fact, even though silent themselves, they can also have quite pretty phonological effects. Consider the relation of 'contraction' that holds between the examples in (12):

12a. I am the greatest
  b. I'm the greatest

Such contraction does not apply blindly; for instance, there is a contrast between (12) and (13):

13a.   John is coming at the same time as I am
  b.   * John is coming at the same time as I'm

Why should (13b) be impossible? The answer relies on the postulation of empty categories: the reason that *I am* cannot contract to *I'm* in (13) is because contraction cannot take place next to an empty category.[3] (13a) is interpreted as shown in the partial analysis in (14):

14.   John is coming at the same time as I am ~~coming~~

and it is the omitted (empty) *coming* that prevents contraction. In case this seems far-fetched, it is worth pointing out that this same explanation accounts for a wide range of other phenomena. A different process, called *wanna*-contraction, is shown in (15):

15a.   I want to go
  b.   I wanna go

This process of contraction too is constrained in interesting ways in that (16a) and (16b) have quite different properties: (16a) is ambiguous, it can mean either that *I want Teddy to succeed* or that *I want to succeed Teddy*. (16b) on the other hand is unambiguous,[4] it has only the latter interpretation *I want to succeed Teddy* – why should this be?

16a.   Teddy is the man I want to succeed
  b.   Teddy is the man I wanna succeed

The analyses shown in (17) suggest why: contraction cannot take place across an empty category, in this instance the trace t_i, so (17a) allows contraction and (17b) does not:

17a.   Teddy$_i$ is the man I want to succeed [t_i]
  b.   Teddy$_i$ is the man I want [t_i] to succeed

In addition to traditional distributional arguments of this kind, there is psycholinguistic evidence for some empty categories, of which the best-known is the 'trace reactivation' effect. Much psycholinguistic work depends on 'priming' experiments: your reaction time to respond to a specific word – for example, *king* – is faster if you have just heard a related word such as *queen* than if you have just heard an unrelated word such as *ink*. In such a situation, *queen* is said to prime *king*. A standard technique for illustrating this phenomenon involves 'cross-modal' priming, where you **hear** a sentence and **see** a probe word to which you have to react as fast as possible. The next step in the argument involves complex examples like (18) (parallel to (10a) *What$_i$ did John put t$_i$ in the wheelbarrow?*). Such sentences exemplify 'filler–gap' dependencies, where the trace or gap relates to the earlier occurrence of *what* or *which boy*:

18. [Which boy]$_i$ did the indulgent grandfather put t$_i$ in the wheelbarrow?

The word *boy* consistently primes the word *girl*, but not a word like *goat*. Accordingly, if you probe immediately after *boy* in (18) you get a facilitatory (speeding-up) effect for the reaction to *girl* but not for the reaction to *goat*. If you probe immediately after *grandfather* the facilitatory effect has disappeared due to the temporal decay of the priming. Remarkably, if you probe immediately after *put* – that is, where the trace of *which boy* is located – the priming effect reappears. The presence of the trace 'reactivates' the priming effect of the lexical item it is linked to. But of course if this explanation is correct the trace – the empty category – must exist (see Swinney and Osterhout, 1990; Love and Swinney, 1996). Not surprisingly the interpretation of these results is controversial (see Ingram and Chenery, in preparation, for discussion), but the form of the argument should be clear.

There are other kinds of empty category and other kinds of argument that could be adduced, but these should suffice to give an intuitive understanding of the nature of the beast. Given such evidence it may seem perverse to say that they don't exist, but many scholars have made precisely that claim and have devised theories in which they play no role. Typical examples are provided by Robin Cooper's (1982) article 'Binding in wholewheat* syntax (*unenriched with inaudibilia)', with the whimsical footnote in the title, or Dick Hudson's (2001:244) blunt claim 'There are no empty categories.'[5] Other authors have argued against particular appeals to empty categories without necessarily throwing out the whole concept, notably Geoff Pullum, with and without the help of Paul Postal (e.g. Pullum, 1997; Postal and Pullum, 1982; etc.). Much of the scepticism about them seems to stem from what Miller (1997:14) refers to as a cast of mind typical of Anglo-Saxon empiricism,[6] but his own position is a more interesting and sustained attempt to demolish the notion by wielding Occam's razor.

William of Occam (or 'Ockham') flourished in the first half of the fourteenth century and was famous for his law of parsimony (*entia non sunt multiplicanda praeter necessitatem*),[7] which decreed that only necessary constructs should be postulated. Miller takes a wide range of phenomena 'explained' by appeal to empty categories (including several of those cited here), provides alternative analyses for them and concludes (with interesting reservations) that empty categories have no role in linguistics.

Even if we grant the success in principle of Miller's enterprise, it is important to note that Occam's razor is a two-edged weapon. In his reanalyses, Miller makes crucial use of theoretical constructs that are not part of the Generativists' ontology, making arguments based on Occam's razor inconclusive. Let's consider just two: the use of 'constructions' and the postulation of Gazdarian 'slash categories'. Constructions, such as the passive construction or the ablative absolute construction, have been around for millennia, but one of the surprising innovations of Chomsky's work is precisely to claim that constructions are just an epiphenomenon: they arise as side-effects of the real primitives of the theory, and hence they have no status in current Minimalism. In brief, the notion 'construction' can be eliminated. If this is correct, then trading empty categories for constructions doesn't look a particularly good bargain. In developing Generalized Phrase Structure Grammar (GPSG: see Gazdar et al., 1985), Gerald Gazdar invented a new kind of category, referred to as a 'slash category' because of the notation used. These new categories were like the old ones except that they had a hole in: so S/NP is a sentence with a missing constituent, specifically a missing NP. The invention was ingenious, and was part of the programme that enabled GPSG to dispense with transformations. But in the present context it is important to note that the trade-off is one between a new kind of 'empty' category, and a new kind of category with something missing. Again, the saving is not obvious.

What is clear is that the explosion in the range of possible descriptive devices that linguists can appeal to has resulted in a situation in which one can do without empty categories. But then one has two responsibilities: first, to show that providing comparably deep explanations for the phenomena observed is possible without using them; second, to show that the resources one is exploiting are not even richer (and hence less desirable) than when using them. Another way of putting this is to say that empty categories are 'theory-dependent' – but they seem to me to be alive and well. I will stop writing about nothing and turn to something a little more tangible – *the*.

Acknowledgement

This chapter has not appeared previously, but part of it was delivered as a lecture ('The necessity for theory') at the ninth conference of the Nordic Association for English Studies, held in Århus, Denmark, in May 2004. I am grateful to the audience for comments and questions.

Notes

1 The Mayans and the Babylonians also seem to have invented zero, but its use in Western science stems from the Sanskrit tradition.
2 The square brackets indicate that the sequence *his grandson*, and not just *grandson*, is the antecedent of the trace.
3 The ungrammaticality of (13b) is probably reducible to the fact that *'m* is necessarily attached to whatever follows it, and here nothing does. See Lightfoot (1999).
4 This is (over-)simplified; for critical discussion, see Pullum and Zwicky (1988, 1992) and the observations below.
5 Hudson has since argued for at least one empty category, 'little' *pro*: see Creider and Hudson (2002).
6 'L'opposition aux morphèmes vides est aussi typique d'une certaine pensée empiriste anglo-saxonne.'
7 Entities should not be multiplied beyond what is necessary.

16

The

It remains to interpret phrases containing the. These are by far the most interesting and difficult.

Bertrand Russell, 'On denoting'

What does *the* mean?

The usual answer that it makes something 'definite' may seem simple, but *the* has many uses that remain obscure on such a definition, and a more adequate response requires a theory. Indeed, if we are going to understand even part of what *the* does we shall require quite a complex theory.

We shall need to appeal to **Syntactic** categories: Nouns, Verbs, clauses, and in particular 'Determiners'. As a special case, we shall need 'empty categories'; that is, categories that have a syntax and a semantics, but are not pronounced. We shall need the idea of hierarchical structure, including the abstract relation known as 'c-command'. We shall need relational notions like 'subject' and 'object' and, as a corollary, the assumption that nouns as well as sentences can have subjects, as in *Marilyn's arrival surprised him*. Subjects and objects are types of 'argument': we shall need these and the claim that some arguments are 'internal' and others 'external'. We shall also need to have recourse to **Semantic** categories or 'types', referring to entities and truth values; and to semantic features like 'definite', 'specific', and others. Part of the reason for this is that while structural notions like (syntactic) subject and object frequently correlate with functional (semantic) notions like agent and patient, they may also dissociate: surface syntax and semantics are not in a one-to-one relation, as shown by the well-known examples *The doctor undertook the operation reluctantly* and *The doctor underwent the operation reluctantly*. In this interface region between syntax and semantics we shall also need to assume a difference between 'arguments' and 'predicates'; and we shall additionally have to appeal to 'licensing' and 'bound variables'. In the process of justifying some of these assumptions we shall also need to refer to **Phonological** categories and processes, such as contraction, because these interact in important ways with syntactic analysis. We shall additionally need to accommodate not only grammatical and interpretable sentences, but also ungrammatical sequences, interpretable or uninterpretable, marked with an asterisk. And we shall need constant recourse to **pragmatics**. (For discussion of all these, cf. Chomsky, 1995a; Radford, 2004a, 2004b; Smith, 2004; and virtually any introduction to linguistics.)

The need for this plethora of theoretical tools may seem implausible if one restricts attention to simple examples. So I'll try to persuade you that they really are necessary by starting with elementary cases and then graduating to more problematic examples.

According to Huddleston and Pullum (2002:368), following a long tradition, the definite article (*the*) is 'the most basic indicator of definiteness', and its use indicates that the referent is 'identifiable'. This works fine for a number of examples: (1a) suggests that one particular (identifiable) spanner is meant, whereas someone who utters (1b) is indifferent to which spanner is supplied.

1a. Bring me the spanner
 b. Bring me a spanner
 c. * Bring me spanner

The ungrammatical (1c) is included to suggest that nouns usually need to be accompanied (licensed) by some article or other determiner if the phrase containing them is to be well-formed. Actually, that's true only of 'count' nouns in the singular, as we can see from (2), and even then there are exceptions, as we shall see below:

2a. Bring me strawberries
 b. Give me beef

The plural in (2a) is fine, even if a little undiscriminating (*Bring me some strawberries* is more plausible), and the 'mass' noun singular in (2b) is grammatically unexceptionable, even if the order sounds a little peremptory. Where a noun can be used indifferently as count or mass, one then has ambiguity: (3) can be construed as corresponding to either of the examples in (4):

3.   Pass me the apple

4a.   Pass me some (e.g. stewed) apple {the only mass of apple that is salient}
 b.   Pass me an apple {the only one which is salient}

Virtually all nouns can be coerced into either usage, so (5) has at least three different interpretations:

5.   Show me penguin

It can be construed either as someone's name, in which case we'd expect (in the written form of English) to have 'Penguin', or as a request made in a restaurant with a somewhat exotic array of food on offer, or of course it could just be ungrammatical.

This 'definite/identifiable' analysis can be easily extended to examples where the definite/indefinite contrast is explicitly played upon, as in (6):

6a.   Maggie looked at the puppy in Peter's pet-shop, but later she decided not to buy a puppy
 b.   Maggie looked at a puppy in Peter's pet-shop, but later she decided not to buy the puppy

As Carol Chomsky, who invented them, puts it, in (6a) 'Maggie saw a particular [that is, "identifiable"] puppy at the shop and later decided not to buy any puppy at all', whereas in (6b) 'Maggie saw a puppy [that is, not marked by the speaker as "identifiable"] at the shop and later decided not to buy that particular puppy' (Chomsky, 1986:334).

There are other uses of *the*, for example with generics, where a whole class is referred to, as in (7), which seem not to be too problematic:

7a.   The dodo is extinct
 b.   The Mauritius dodo is extinct

But things become a little more difficult for 'identifiability' with idiosyncratic examples where the presence or absence of *the* seems to make no difference to the meaning, as in (8):

8a. Swallows arrive in spring/swallows arrive in the spring
  b. Conrad has become treasurer/Conrad has become the treasurer

or where the article does not suggest that something is definite but rather indicates a subtle distinction between an activity carried out as a profession and as an idle pursuit, as in (9):

9a. Igor plays the violin when he is depressed
  b. Igor plays violin in the Philharmonia Orchestra

Omitting *the* in (9a) results in a feeling of oddness – it seems as though he is changing his profession to cure his mood; inserting *the* in (9b) is acceptable but seems faintly condescending, as though the violinist were not quite a professional. The identifiability of the violin in question seems equally irrelevant in both. Such examples as (8) and (9) may nonetheless provide grist for the theoretical mill. Huddleston and Pullum (2002:409) observe that 'bare' NPs like *treasurer* in (8b), which express a 'role', are 'invariably definite', and hence are 'invariably replaceable by their counterparts with determiner *the*'. Such replaceability reinforces the generalization made with regard to (1c) that nouns like to be accompanied by determiners, and when they are not one might well be tempted to postulate a phonologically silent one.

There are still other 'adverbial' uses of *the*, especially in superlatives like (10):

10. All the students did rather badly, but Doreen made (the) most mistakes

In (10) the article is again optional, its presence or absence making little difference to the interpretation of the sentence as a whole, and identifiability again being irrelevant.

All such examples are well known and, relatively well understood, even if 'the' meaning of *the* is yet to emerge. But I want to concentrate on a phenomenon, illustrated in (11) and (12), which fits less obviously under any such account:

11a. My brother is in **charge** of this man
  b. My brother is in **control** of this man

12a. My brother is in **the charge** of this man
  b. My brother is in **the control** of this man

In (11) *my brother* is the agent and *this man* is the patient of the 'being in charge/control' relation; in (12) the roles are reversed: *my brother* is the patient and *this man* is the agent. It's clear that *charge* and *control* are not being differentially 'identified' in such cases, so how can we account for this pattern? Which bits of our theoretical armamentarium do we need in order to make sense of the alternation?

The common response that the examples are simply 'idiomatic' won't do. If there were a single such example, it might indeed be true that we could do no more than list the two usages with and without *the* as arbitrary facts about the lexical entry of, say, *charge*. However, (11) and (12) together make it implausible that we are dealing with an unpredictable, non-compositional, idiom, and there are anyway many similar examples, such as those in (13) and (14):

13a. The knight was in **sight** of the dragon when he fell off his horse
  b. The knight was in **the sight** of the dragon when he fell off his horse

14a. The slimy monster was in **reach** of Beowulf when it plunged into the abyss
  b. The slimy monster was in **the reach** of Beowulf when it plunged into the abyss

In (13a) the knight can (potentially) see the dragon;[1] in (13b) the dragon can see the knight; in (14a) the monster could reach Beowulf, in (14b) Beowulf could reach the monster. In each case the thematic roles of the protagonists are reversed. Related, but slightly different, examples show the same kind of switch, as seen in (15), with the interpretation given in (15'):

15a. In **view** of Saddam, we had better invade
  b. In **the view** of Saddam, we had better invade

15a'. Given our perspective on Saddam, we had better invade
   b'. Given Saddam's perspective on us, we had better invade

So what do we need, apart from the mention of subject, object, thematic role, and so on? The first point to notice is that in all these examples the **bold** NP, with or without the definite article, is part of a predicate, not an argument (cf. Bowers, 2001). That is, [in reach of Beowulf] performs the same sort of semantic function as [slimy], which tells us something about the monster. The difference between arguments and predicates can be illustrated by means of a pair such as (16):

16a. I found Tom a good doctor (when he had a heart condition)
   b. I found Tom (to be) a good doctor (when I had a heart condition)

In (16a) *a good doctor* is a third argument of the verb *find* (*Tom* and *I* are the other two), whereas in (16b) the same sequence picks out not a third argument – another person – but predicates a property of Tom. This relation is characteristically highlighted by the presence of *be*, though the fact that *be* is optional in (16b) indicates that this is not necessary, but it is clearly not insignificant that all of (11–14) contain some form of the verb *be*.

The relevance of this distinction between arguments and predicates is that they have different properties, and the interpretation of an NP (when preceded by *the*) as 'identifiable' pertains only to NPs which are arguments. As is indicated by the pair in (17), the difference is not only in semantic interpretation, but there are also syntactic differences: predicates, as in (17a), and arguments, as in (17b), allow differential extraction:

17a. Which mountain was Tenzing [the first man to climb *t*]?
   b. *Which mountain did you meet [the first man to climb *t*]?[2]

The second point to note is that, because the *of* phrase varies as underlying object of *charge* (in 11) and as subject of *charge* (in 12), there is alternation with an overt possessive for (12) – but not (11):

18. My brother is in this man's charge

That is, we regularly have alternations of the kind given in (19), where possession can be coded either by a prepositional phrase (*the love of God*) or by the possessive '*s* (*God's love*). Only the former of these is ambiguous, with *God* as either subject or object; the latter has only a subject interpretation:

19a.   The love of God protects us/is a sign of our wisdom
  b.   God's love protects us/?is a sign of our wisdom

This makes it plausible that (12a) (My brother is in **the charge** of this man) is more closely related to (18) than is (11a) (My brother is in **charge** of this man) and probably derives from (18) by a movement rule.

   The third piece of equipment we need to draw from our theoretical arsenal pertains to empty categories of the sort we looked at in the previous chapter. The most frequent situation is that nouns are preceded by some kind of determiner without which the noun is not licensed. That is, the oddity of (1c) and (5) is attributed to the fact that the noun (*spanner* or *penguin*) has nothing to license it. Given that (11), with the bare singular *charge* or *control*, is well-formed, the assumption is that it must have been licensed. One obvious possibility is a null (empty) possessive, of the kind also found in (20) (see Chierchia, 1998):

20a.   John has gone to bed
  b.   John has gone to school

Examples like these allow alternants with a determiner, either *his* or *the*,[3] as in (21):

21a.   John has gone to his bed
  b.   John has gone to the school

These alternants do not have the same interpretation as (20), where the implication is that he has gone to bed to get in it and go to sleep, or he has gone to school for the usual purpose of study or whatever. But in the absence of explicit cancellation, they do imply that he has gone to his own (identifiable) bed or his usual (identifiable) school. The conclusion is that *bed* and *school* in (20) are in fact preceded and licensed by an empty determiner, and in particular, a null possessive.

The fourth piece of theoretical equipment we need is the idea of a 'bound variable', and the condition on such entities that they have to be 'c-commanded' (in the sense described in detail in the introduction) by some antecedent. The difference between a bound variable pronoun and an 'ordinary' (referential) pronoun is illustrated in (22):

22a.   I like his father
  b.   Everyone likes his father

In (22a) *his* simply picks out some individual who would normally be identifiable from the context. (22b) has the same possible interpretation, but it has an additional reading on which each individual subsumed by *everyone* likes his own respective father. This is the bound variable interpretation of *his*, and it is usually the case that such a bound variable must be c-commanded by its antecedent (*everyone*), hence the unacceptability of (23), where this condition is not satisfied:

23.   Every Englishman's mother likes his father

That is, (23) allows only an interpretation corresponding to that of (22a) and not one corresponding to (22b) – it is, surprisingly, unambiguous. This is because *every Englishman* in (23) does not c-command *his father*, so the bound variable reading is excluded.

The fifth piece of machinery we need is the notion 'external argument'. Simple transitive verbs like *love* take two arguments, a subject and an object, where the object is 'internal' to the Verb Phrase, and the subject is 'external' to the Verb Phrase. A glance at the tree in example (22) of the introduction (*My friend likes the penguins*) will show that the object NP is inside (immediately dominated by) VP, whereas the subject is outside (above) the VP. Intransitive verbs – that is, those with only one argument – may have that argument underlyingly either internal or external to the VP.[4] So a verb like *laugh* has only an external argument, whereas a verb like *sink* has only an internal argument, resulting in a range of syntactic differences between the two classes. (For discussion, see e.g. Baltin, 2001; Bowers, 2001.)

It is time to recapitulate. We need, (relatively) uncontroversially, to make all the assumptions in (24):

24a.   *Charge, control, sight,* and so on, like all nouns, must have a determiner.
  b.   The null possessive is a determiner (i.e. an empty category).
  c.   It is a bound variable pronoun, so that it needs a c-commanding antecedent.
  d.   Nouns like *charge* must have an external argument in the syntax. In (11) the external argument is *My brother.*

This agglomeration of theoretical claims is not yet an explanation for the interpretation of the presence or absence of the definite article in (11) and (12), but it lays the groundwork for any such account. Even this is not quite true: it allows such a basis except for the definiteness of the article in (12): that is, why we have (12a) *My brother is in **the charge** of this man,* rather than the impossible (25):

25.   My brother is in **a charge** of this man

Even this can be made to follow from independently motivated properties of possessives, of the kind seen in (26):

26a.   He broke the/?a leg of a table
  b.   He was shot in the/*an arm

(26a) *He broke the leg of a table* has the interpretation that *He broke a leg of a table* would have were it fully felicitous. Similarly, *the* in (26b) does not identify the arm that 'he' was shot in; that is irrelevant. That is, the (syntactic) definiteness is 'superficial', in that such phrases may be *semantically* definite or indefinite.

So I haven't answered the question at the beginning,[5] but the wealth of interrelations illustrated here gives one hope that an answer is feasible. That may look superficially like a pyrrhic victory, so two final observations are in order by way of an 'envoi'. First, small puzzles need an unexpectedly rich theory for their solution, and looking for such solutions may shed light in dark corners. Second, depth of analysis (hence the complexity of analysis) is a positive feature, not a negative feature. It is, surprisingly, desirable that the structure postulated for even a simple sentence should be extremely complex, because it makes explicit the range of predictions that can in principle falsify your position. More prosaically, to explain any of the minutiae of language, you need to consider (almost) everything.[6] Finally, think of the problem children face in mastering this panoply of facts. How do they acquire the difference between (11) and (12)? It seems unlikely that the adult knowledge we all share about them is specific to these particular examples, but piecemeal development of bits of the armamentarium suggested here begins to make the task a little less intractable. They come to the task well prepared with prior knowledge.

Acknowledgements

Part of this chapter was delivered as a lecture ('The necessity for theory') at the ninth conference of the Nordic Association for English Studies, held in Århus, Denmark, in May 2004. I am grateful to the audience for useful comments, and to Amahl Smith and Ivan Smith for discussion of some of the examples. My main debt is to Annabel Cormack, who provided much of the basis for an explanation. I am grateful to Junji Hamamatsu for drawing to my attention a paper by Tom Roeper (2000) which discusses a range of comparable examples. I have not been able to take account of it here.

The has been a major focus of attention in the philosophy of language at least since Russell's (1905) paper but, as Jerry Fodor whimsically put it, 'Early in the century there was detectable optimism about the prospects for analysing "the", but it faded' (Fodor, 2004:17).

Notes

1 For some speakers, (13a) is ambiguous with the reading I have indicated, plus the reading I give for (13b) as a 'poetic alternant'. For me, both are univocal with the readings shown. For others, the examples are marginal. If I am right about the complexity of the theoretical machinery needed to approach an explanation of the facts, such variation is not surprising (see chapter 12 above for relevant discussion).

2 The *t* is an empty category, specifically a *trace*. See the introduction and chapter 15 above for more gory details.

3 In general, pronouns pattern like determiners, as in *They saw the linguists/us linguists*.

4 The claim is, of course, controversial. For some, it would be less so if one replaced VP by V-bar; for others that would be equally controversial. The details are irrelevant to the current discussion.

5   And there are still mysteries galore, such as why you can have an ellip-
     tical form *Fred's in charge*, parallel to *Fred's in charge of the prisoner*, but
     no **Fred's in the charge* parallel to *Fred's in the charge of the prisoner*.
6   In this respect, generative grammar bears out the structuralist dictum
     that language is a system in which everything hangs together
     ('chaque langue forme un système où tout se tient'), attributed to each
     of Meillet and de Saussure.

17

Are Gucks Mentally Represented?

guck *(noun) – A foolish saying.*

Oxford English Dictionary

It is a commonplace that little children mispronounce the words of the language they are exposed to, so that a two-year-old learning English might produce 'duck' as [gʌk], 'blue' as [bu:], and 'banana' as [ba:nə]. It is equally clear that the relation between the adult and child forms is systematic and predictable: given that the child pronounces 'feet' as [wi:t], 'finger' as [wiŋə], and 'fire' as [wæ:], it is no surprise to discover that he pronounces 'fork' as [wɔ:k]. In other words, the child's production is rule-governed. There is also good evidence that such mispronunciations are not an accurate reflection of the child's perceptual abilities, and that the child's lexical representations are in most respects equivalent to the adult surface forms (see e.g. Smith, 1973).

That perception is in advance of production is obvious from a range of phenomena: for instance, the child can successfully discriminate minimal pairs where it can pronounce neither of the forms concerned. At a stage when he pronounced both 'mouth' and 'mouse' as [maut], my son Amahl consistently identified pictures of mouths and mice correctly. More strikingly, as a result of the kind of regular rules just alluded to, he pronounced 'puddle' as [pʌgəl], but 'puzzle' as [pʌdəl], so the reason for the mispronunciation of 'puddle' couldn't be his inability to say it.

How to explain these asymmetries is controversial, and a variety of suggestions have appeared in the literature. These include the claim that the child has two grammars (Hayes, 2004), or two lexicons (Menn and Matthei, 1992); that it has to unlearn innate constraints (Stampe, 1969); that its lexical representations are seriously under-specified (Ingram, 1974); that it is indulging in constraint re-ranking of the kind exploited in Optimality Theory (Gnanadesikan, 1995; Smolensky, 1996; Tesar and Smolensky, 2000); and so on.

My own contribution, long ago, was to argue (Smith, 1973) for the existence and psychological reality of an ordered set of 'realization rules' that took the adult surface form as input and gave the child's pronunciation as output. A typical example of such a derivation is provided by the sequence below, converting 'squat' to [gɔp]:

a. /skwɔt/ becomes |skwɔp|
   (harmonizing a coronal consonant to a preceding labialized sequence /kw/)
b. |skwɔp| becomes |kwɔp|
   (deleting pre-consonantal /s/)
c. |kwɔp| becomes |kɔp|
   (deleting post-consonantal sonorants)
d. |kɔp| becomes [gɔp]
   (neutralizing the voicing distinction between /k/ and /g/).

Various people were unhappy with the apparently baroque complexity of this suggestion (one of the two dozen rules I postulated contained over twenty distinctive feature specifications). As Gnanadesikan (1995:26–7) put it: 'Using this model has the unsatisfactory result that the child has more phonological rules than the adults do . . . rules for which he has never received any evidence. Also . . . many of these rules have the same purpose. For example, seven of 23 rules have the function of eliminating consonant clusters.'

I agree that this complexity may seem counter-intuitive, but I am unhappy with all the current alternative solutions. In particular, I am not persuaded by either of the Optimality-Theoretic claims that 'what differs between "production" and "comprehension" is only *which structures compete*; structures that share the same underlying form in the former case, structures that share the same surface form in the latter case' (Smolensky, 1996:722–3.); or that 'grammars are parallel optimisations over structural descriptions containing both input and surface forms' (Smolensky, 1996: 729–30), with the corollary that: 'if grammars are sets of parametrised inviolable constraints, it is difficult to see how, with a single grammar, children could display one set of parameter settings in their productions, while correctly processing adult forms requiring different settings' (p. 730).

The issue may seem infantile but, if it can be used to provide an argument for Optimality Theory (OT) over Principles and Parameters Theory (P&P), it is clearly important; especially as all current theories are so powerful that such evidence is notoriously hard to find. For example, in both approaches the child's task is facilitated by the presumed availability of a universal set of antecedently given possibilities: in P&P it has to select the appropriate values from a set of binary choices, whereas in OT the task is to determine the language-specific hierarchy of the violable constraints. There are of course other differences, as even within OT the initial ranking is controversial: Gnanadesikan (1995) proposes that in the child's initial state the markedness constraints outrank faithfulness constraints; whereas Tesar and Smolensky (2000) assume that all constraints are initially unranked.

What is common to both positions, and to all the others mentioned, is the assumption that the child's inputs and outputs define levels of representation which are comparable in status. For instance, Hayes (2004:191) suggests that children construct a production phonology that maps adult surface forms onto their own, simpler, output representations; and Menn and Matthei claim (1992:243) that both input and output forms are 'stored', tacitly ascribing psychological reality to them and the rules or processes that produce them. I have a different suggestion: the child's output forms are simply not 'represented' at all, and the realization rules have no psychological status. Indeed, given the child's lexical representations, the realization rules must be in some sense independent of competence. I suggest – with caveats – that they have a status comparable to that of the motoric processes that give rise to the slight (but consistent) allophonic effects such as the difference in the length of a vowel before /n/ or /d/. The only psychologically real entities for the child are the adult forms that constitute its lexical representations; its own pronunciations are then the result of the operation of a (connectionist) neural network which yields the appropriate outputs. But these outputs do not define a level of representation.

I should emphasize that this proposal does not mark a connectionist conversion (see Smith, 1997). I am claiming (only) that (only) the realization rules are replaced by a neural network – everything else remains 'symbolic'. The diachronic development of the child's production is then a function of biological maturation, giving rise to the apparently increasing complication of the phonological system (cf. e.g. Dinnsen, 1992; Kent, 1992).

This suggestion is reminiscent of Stemberger's claim that 'the child has no overt procedures for adapting perceived forms to a form that he or she can produce' (1992:166), but there are crucial differences. The consistency of the child's production makes it implausible that its pronunciations are simply 'errors of access' to the lexical representation as Stemberger claims (1992:185), and I deny the parallelism between lexical representations and the 'output states' which he says are 'accessible', because – for me – the 'output patterns' have no status. There are also parallels with any framework which 'derives phonetic forms as adaptations to universal performance constraints' (e.g. Lindblom, 1992:135). But Lindblom's use of an analysis-by-synthesis approach with a feedback loop is fatally flawed in that it predicts that the child will get perennially and permanently stuck with 'puzzles' (see Morton and Smith, 1974).

Supposing it is possible to construct an appropriate network (my connectionist friends could do it in their sleep), are there problems with the suggestion? The putative existence of 'production schemata', 'templates' or 'idiosyncratic strategies' might suggest that the child is manipulating the output forms (see Vihman, 1996), but I don't think this is true: no further process or rule of the phonology ever needs to refer to such entities, so they have no formal status, and their properties should fall out automatically from the connectionist architecture.

A more serious problem arises if the child can monitor its own production, suggesting that this output is psychologically real. In essence, this amounts to the question of whether you can 'meta-represent' a non-representation. Consider an example. When he was two and a half years old I had the following conversation with Amahl, as I was puzzled by his ability to pronounce the nasal in 'hand', but apparently not that in 'jump' (Smith, 1973:10):

Me:	Say 'jump'
A:	[dʌp]
Me:	No, 'jump'
A:	[dʌp]
Me:	No, 'jummmp'
A:	Only Daddy can say [dʌp]

It is clear that his final [dʌp] is intended to represent the adult form 'jump', or it just wouldn't be true. But equally it looks as if he is referring indirectly to his own pronunciation, as otherwise the remark makes no sense. But referring to his own output is precisely what he ought not to be able to do if it is really not represented and has no status. Fortunately, there is a way out: any processing model must contain a response buffer in which there is an 'echo' of the preceding few seconds' exchange, and it is this, rather than any encoded representation, which is used to monitor one's own output. Such echoic monitoring could also account for whatever 'repairs' take place in child language and, despite Clark's (2003:144) remark that such self-corrections appear from age one onwards, I suspect that they do not appear systematically until the age of three or so: after the majority of childhood mispronunciations have disappeared.

There remains the problem of motivating the details of the neural net I have postulated. Some of them are simply a reflection of the child's inability to pronounce some sounds – [z], for example; but 'puzzles' show that that is not the whole story. My original realization rules accounted for this motoric inability in terms of context-free rules which simply neutralized adult contrasts. Crucially, these were preceded by a number of context-sensitive rules that effected consonant harmony, cluster reduction, and similar processes. The former are the result of the immaturity of the motor system; the latter are somewhat mysterious, but probably arise from formal properties of the network. I'm not enough of a neural networker to prove this, but I'm sure there are connectionists out there who would be happy to help me prove that gucks are *not* mentally represented.

Acknowledgement

A version of this chapter appeared originally in 2003 in *Glot International* 7:164–6.

Further reading

For further discussion, see Smith (2003b) and the postscript below.

Postscript: A Refutation?

This speculation about mental representation was met by a deafening silence. Friends and colleagues were kind enough to say it sounded plausible, even that it solved – in the spirit of Minimalism – a long-standing problem, but no one tried to make it work. Maybe someone should try: there is a serious potential problem for the position I put forward, casting it into serious doubt, though I shall attempt to defend it. The challenge comes, appropriately enough, from the metalinguistic abilities of Amahl's own son, Zachary ('Z' hereafter; see also chapter 8), at the age of three. I have been studying Z systematically since he began to babble at the age of nine months or so. At three years he had a phonological inventory consisting of about fifteen consonants – viz.: /p, t, ʔ, b, d, f, s, h, v, z, m, n, r, l, w/ – and most of the adult vowels. That is, his system was lacking the adult velars /k, g, ŋ/ and also /j, θ, ð, tʃ, dʒ/. /ʃ/ and /ʒ/ were beginning to appear, but were not yet stable, and /ð/ occurred somewhat sporadically. In word-initial position he had clusters consisting of an obstruent followed by /r/: specifically, /pr, br, tr, dr, fr, sr/. The phonetic realization of these clusters occasionally had [l] in place of /r/, but there was no consistent contrast, and /tr/ for instance did duty for a wide range of adult combinations (/tr, kr, kl, tʃ, str, skr, tw, kw/) as shown in (1):

1. trein   – train, crane
    traim   – climb
    trɛ: – chair
    traips   – stripes
    ʌn'tru: – unscrew
    trɛnti: – twenty
    traiʔ   – quite

His reduction of clusters beginning with /s/ was usually as expected, with examples as in (2), but there were some (consistent) surprises,[1] as illustrated in (3):

2. pænə   – spanner
    tˤəuʔin   – stroking
    ta:vin   – starving
    tɔtlənd   – Scotland

3. sɛl   – smell
    saiu   – smile
    sɔləud   – swallowed
    si:z   – sneeze

So much by way of background. When he was three years and nineteen days we had the following exchange. He had asked for [sæmbəl ɛd] (scrambled egg) for his tea and, on being asked to repeat it, came out moments later with [træmbəld ɛd]. He then spontaneously volunteered: [it bi'dinz wið 'tʳ'] – 'it begins with [tʳ]' (with a faint schwa offglide).[2] Over a period of some days, I then asked him what a whole series of words began with, eliciting the forms illustrated in (4). The left-hand column is the stimulus I gave him, the middle column is his response, and the right-hand column is his normal pronunciation of the word:

4a. fork   – [fə]   fɔ:ʔ
     foot   – [fə]   fut
     Mummy   – [mə]   mʌmi:
     Daddy   – [də]   dædi:

 b. sheep   – [ʃ]   si:p *or* ʃi:p
     sleeve   – [ʃ]   si:v *or* ʃi:v

 c. Grandpa   – [drə]   dræmpa:
     Josh(ua)   – [drə]   drɔs *or* dʒɔʃ
     train   – [tʳə]   trein
     crane   – [tʳə]   trein
     yellow   – [lə]   lɛləu

 d. piece   – [pʰə]   pi:s
     spoon   – [pʰə]   pu:n
     before   – [fə]   ə'fɔ:
     egg   – [ə]   ɛd

In these and further exchanges over the next few weeks, I obtained a further sixty or so examples illustrating the same phenomenon. For those who wish to pursue the correct interpretation of these data, I give a complete list at the end of this postscript, including those where he was less than consistent in his offerings. Acquisitional data are rarely, if ever, unproblematic.

One of the more interesting aspects of his performance was his spontaneous production of new examples for me, volunteering, for instance, that *plant*, [praːnt] in his pronunciation, begins with [pr], or that [pɔt biˈdinz wið ə pə, lait pɔpiː] – ' " pot" begins with a [pə] like "poppy"'.[3] A few examples are given in (5):

5a. trein biˈdinz wið [tʳə] ən bɔʔs biˈdinz wið [bə] dʒʌs laiʔ bɔtəl
   'train' begins with [tr] and 'box' begins with [b] just like 'bottle'

b. He said explicitly that 'sleep' and 'sheep' are the same when he says them ([ʃiːp]), and different when I do. At first he said they were different for him until he tried saying them slowly. Later he experimented with 'squash' and 'cloth' (both [trɔs] or [trɔʃ] for him), and said that I say them differently but he says them the same, after practising both *sotto voce* or in a whisper.

c. Playing 'I spy' (at his instigation) I said: 'I spy . . . something beginning with [dʒ]', making it clear that I was intending Joshua (his baby brother). His reaction was: [drɔs biˈdinz wið ə drə, lait drimiː ən dræmpaː] – ' "Josh" begins with [dr] like "Jimmy" and "Grandpa".' Similarly, 'grape' begins with a [dr] – just like 'Josh', 'John' and 'Grandpa'.

There are several different kinds of data: the simplest, and least illuminating, are where his and the adult pronunciations are the same: examples like *fork*, *piece*, *Mummy*, and so on. More interesting are those where there is a difference in the pronunciation, but Z is incapable of pronouncing the correct adult form: examples like *Grandpa*, *crane*, *yellow*, and so on. Here what is of greatest interest is his linking together of words with different adult pronunciations in a single class (*train* and *crane*, for instance), and his awareness that this linking was not valid for me (*play* and *pray*, for instance). Of most interest are those examples where there is a difference in the pronunciation, and Z **is** capable of pronouncing the (initial element of the) adult form: examples like *spoon* and *Scoop*, where he is certainly able to pronounce [s]; and *before* and *potato*, where he can produce the correct consonant ('b' or 'p') in stressed syllables (and occasionally in unstressed syllables).

A complicating factor is that, in these examples, it seems that he is treating the adult initial **sequence** as a unit. That is, for Z, '*frog*' and '*farm*', or '*spoon*' and '*soon*', do not begin alike. *Spoon* begins for him not with the segment /s/ but the complex unit |sp| with no internal structure (as yet).[4] There are two kinds of confirmation of this suggestion. First is the development of phonetically accurate clusters of consonant + /r/ which preceded, and hence seemed to be independent of, the development of a phonetically accurate rendition of /r/ itself. Second is his treatment of *piano* (and other items) as seen in the following exchange. I began by saying: 'I spy with my little eye something beginning with [pʰə]', and when Z gave no response, I said 'piano' (which he was thumping at the time). He immediately responded with: prænəu bi'dinz wiv ə [pʳə] ('*piano* begins with a "pr"'), apparently correcting me. Adult initial clusters, undifferentiated in Z's production (see (1) above), are treated not as clusters but as units.

What is strikingly clear from the overwhelming majority of these examples is that Z is showing metalinguistic awareness of his own pronunciation of these words. There is no doubt that he can hear the difference between the various possible pairs that he pronounces identically – *train* and *crane*, for instance, as he was able instantly to identify the correct toy from my pronunciation. It is also clear that he is in some cases able to pronounce the 'correct' initial consonant he has just been exposed to: *spoon* begins with an 's', which is phonetically extremely close to the [s] he produces at the beginning of his pronunciation of *sneeze*. Moreover, he was able to recognize whether two items began with the same sound in either my or his own pronunciation, (e.g. *cow* and *cupboard*), even if he was somewhat reticent about revealing his productive limitations, as seen in:

NVS: Do 'crane' and 'train' begin with the same sound?

Z: No. I'm not going to tell you what [trein ən trein] begin with

There are (at least) three possibilities: first, the idea I toyed with earlier, he can meta-represent a non-representation; second, he is using a response buffer like an echo-box to recapitulate the sounds he produces; third, the output form the child produces does have status as a level of representation. The first of these still seems inherently implausible, maybe incoherent. The second may also be problematic, but can perhaps be rescued. On several occasions Z instantly responded 'No' to questions like 'Do *train* and *crane* begin the same?', but after a little cogitation changed that answer to 'Yes'. The initial negative response could be due to the effect of the response buffer maintaining an echo of my pronunciation, with his positive follow-up reaction being the result of his consulting his own intuitions, suggesting that his own pronunciation must be represented, contrary to my original speculation. However, this is not a necessary conclusion: the 'representations' under discussion are transient, and not part of the represented grammar. If his metalinguistic awareness involves representations of items in the buffer which have been subject to his realization rules, his output forms are not mentally represented in the strict sense defined by grammatical theory. Not only do we not need to define a level of representation in the buffer, it would be a confusion of competence and performance to try to do so.

So what is the take-home message? For Zachary, and presumably for children in general, the output form has no status as a level of representation, but is accessible to sometimes conscious introspection in virtue of being a product of the response buffer. My criticisms of the various positions in the literature were correct and we can simplify the structure of the grammar in line with the tenets of current Minimalism. Gucks are not mentally represented.

Can that really be right . . . ?

Inventory of Zachary's judgements of what various words begin with

As in the text above, the left-hand column is the stimulus I gave him (except where he volunteered the information), the middle column is his response, and the right-hand column is his normal pronunciation of the word. The degree of aspiration of voiceless plosives was inconsistent. Where several entries occur for the same word this simply records different utterances of the same item (in chronological order).

Amahl	– [ə]	'æmɑ:l
Anne	– [ə]	æn

He volunteered that '*Amahl* and *Anne* begin the same with [ə].' These are the names of his parents.

before	– [fə]	əˈfɔ:
bottle	– [bɔʔ]	bɔtəl *or* bɔʔəl
box	– [bə]	bɔʔs
bread	– [dʳə]	brɛd

When I denied it he gave: [bʳə].

chair	– [tr]	trɛ:
climb	– [trˀ]	traim
cloth	– [tʳə]	trɔʃ
cow	– [pʰə]	tau

When asked again, he managed [thə], and then volunteered: [thə] fə tau ən tʌbəd; that is, [thə] for *cow* and *cupboard* (his pronunciation is [tʌbəd]).

crane	– [tʳə]	trein
cupboard	– [thə]	tʌbəd See 'cow'
Daddy	– [də]	dædi:
drum	– [dr]	drʌm

When asked: 'Is that the same as "duck"?', he replied: No.

egg	– [ə]	ɛd
equipment	– [trˀ]	tripmənt
farm	– [fə]	fa:m
fire	– [fə]	fæ:
flapjack	– [ʃ]	læpdzæʔ *or* ʃæpdʒæʔ
		or fʳæpdzæʔ
foot	– [fə]	fut
fork	– [fə]	fɔ:ʔ
frame	– [frə]	freim
France	– [frə]	fra:ns
frog	– [frə]	frɔd

Explicitly not the same as 'farm'.

funny	– [fə]	fʌni:

Explicitly not the same as 'France'.

giraffe	– [dr]	dra:f
girl	– [də]	də:l
Grandma	– [drə]	drænma:

Grandpa	– [drə]	dræmpa:
Gruff	– [drə]	drʌf
grape	– [dr]	dreip
hand	– [fə]	hænd

When asked again, he managed [hə].

ice-cream	– [ais]	'aistri:m
Jimmy	– [drə]	drimi:
Josh	– [drə]	drɔs *or* dʒɔʃ
Josh	– [dʒə]	drɔs *or* dʒɔʃ
Josh	– [dʒrˀ]	drɔs *or* dʒɔʃ
Joshua	– drɔsu:a: bi'dinz wið ə dʒəˀ⁵	
kettle	– [tə]	tètul See 'tomato'
Mummy	– [mə]	mʌmi:
nose	– [nˀ]	nəuz
piano	– [pʳə]	prænəu
piece	– [pʰə]	pi:s
plant	– [pr]	pra:nt
play	– [pr]	prei
poppy	– [p]	pɔpi:
pot	– [p]	pɔt
potato	– [tə]	teitəu
pray	– [pr]	prei
room	– [rˀ]	rum
Scoop	– [tʰə]	tu:p
scrambled	– [tr]	træmbəld
sheep	– [ʃ]	si:p *or* ʃi:p
sleep	– [ʃ]	ʃi:p
sleep	– [ə ʃə]	ʃi:p
sleeve	– [ʃ]	si:v *or* ʃi:v
sleeve	– [ʃˀ]	ʃi:v
sneeze	– [ə si:]	si:z

He prefixed several of his answers with a schwa that I interpreted as an indefinite article.

sorry	– [sˀ]	sɔi:
spoon	– [pʰə]	pu:n
squash	– [tʳə]	trɔʃ
stool	– [tʰə]	tu:l
strong	– [trˀ]	trɔn *or* (once) srɔn
swans	– [ʃ]	ʃɔnz
swimming	– [ʃ]	ʃimin
swing	– [s]	sʷin

thanks	– [s]	sænts
think	– [ə sˀ]	sint
think	– [sˀ]	sin?

He volunteered: 'Just like "sorry".'

| three | – [frə] | fri: |

He volunteered: 'Just like "frame".'

| tomato | – [tə] | ma: təu |

Repeated [tə] when questioned. He then volunteered: ə tɛtul bi'dinz wið ə 'tə' – a *kettle* begins with a [tə].

NS (holding up a tomato):	What does this begin with?
Z:	[ma:]
NS:	And when I say it?
Z (sotto voce):	[tə'ma:təu] pause: [tə'ma:]

torch	– [tˀ]	tɔ:s
train	– [tʳə]	trein
yawn	– 'don't know'	lɔ:n
yawn	– [lə]	lɔ:n
yellow	– [lə]	lɛləu
your	– 'don't know'	ɔ:
Zachary	– [zə]	'zæ?əri:

Acknowledgement

This potential, but hopefully failed, refutation of my earlier claim was presented at the Advanced Core Training in Linguistics lecture series at UCL in November 2004. I am grateful to the audience for a number of helpful criticisms and suggestions, though they are, of course, absolved of responsibility.

Further reading

I should perhaps have couched my discussion of the 'response buffer' in terms of the 'phonological loop' (in particular, the 'phonological output buffer') made famous in Alan Baddeley's work: see, for instance,. Baddeley (2003).

Notes

1   I was surprised because his father had reduced such clusters to the sonorant rather than the /s/. I shouldn't have been surprised, as in each case Z was preserving the element lower on the sonority hierarchy.

2   It transpired that his father had been playing 'I spy' with him – using the format 'I spy with my little eye something beginning with [pʰə].' Z had not previously volunteered such information.

3   Such examples illustrate his general metalinguistic awareness and may be a function, at least in part, of his unusual phonological inventory (in particular the absence of velars). This is exemplified in the following: Z said something about [dra:s] ('glass'), but I misunderstood what he was saying, and asked if he meant 'grass'. He replied: [nəu dra:s, laiʔ windəuz a: meid ɔv] – 'No, "glass" like windows are made of.'

4   This has in fact been suggested as the correct analysis even for the adult language; cf., for example, Fudge (1969:273). As far as I know, no one suggests that /pr/ or /fr/ are phonological units in the same way.

5   This was a striking example of a mismatch between use and mention.

18

Wonder

. . . wonder (which is the seed of knowledge) is an impression of pleasure in itself.

Francis Bacon, *Advancement of Learning.*

My earliest memory is one of wonder. I was falling over but never hit the ground: my mother had deftly pulled on the toddler harness I was wearing and stopped me in mid-air. I have never forgotten the sight of the ground rushing towards me, and not hitting me. For Plato, 'wonder is the only beginning of philosophy', and for Descartes it is 'the first of all the passions', epitomized in our reaction to the rainbow (Fisher, 1998:41–5). But wonder is an emotion, and there has been an unfortunate tendency to equate the emotional with the irrational, and dismiss it from scientific consideration. As a result of looking at an unusual case of Asperger's syndrome (Smith et al., 2003), I have been wondering where the emotions fit in a theory of the mind. Has preoccupation with the purely rational prevented us from understanding cognition more generally? Is the divorce between rationality and emotion implicit in that question itself pernicious? Is it time to return to our philosophical forebears and try to integrate the emotions into our theories of the mind?

Asperger's syndrome is standardly viewed as a form of autism, characterized both developmentally and in the adult steady state by 'impairments of the development of social interaction, communication and imagination' (Wing, 1991:111). In turn, the basic aetiology of autism has, for the last twenty years or so, been located in a defective Theory of Mind (see e.g. Baron-Cohen, 1995). This deficiency explains why sufferers fail some false-belief tasks (the standard criterion for a defective Theory of Mind), and may contribute to their social ineptitude, though it is independent of their normal, or even elevated, intelligence. It has been further suggested that deaf children's impaired understanding of emotions is attributable to 'an impaired theory of mind' (Rieffe and Terwogt 2000:601), and that a comparable deficit underlies Asperger's subjects' characteristic difficulty in interpreting emotions, especially from facial expressions (Tantam, 1991:158).

That this constellation of social, emotional and cognitive problems is **typical** of Asperger's subjects is not at issue, but the question arises whether the syndrome is correctly characterized by their individual necessity and joint sufficiency. Is a deficit in Theory of Mind necessary for the correct ascription of Asperger's syndrome? My understanding of the literature is that this is indeed normally assumed. For instance, Frith (1991:21) writes: 'well adapted Asperger Syndrome individuals may have all the trappings of socially adapted behaviour, may have learnt to solve belief attribution problems, but may yet not have a normally functioning theory of mind'.

The case mentioned above casts such an assumption into doubt, as it seems that these characteristic properties may dissociate: in particular, Theory of Mind may be intact in someone with all the other manifestations of Asperger's syndrome. KH is an eleven-year-old boy diagnosed with Asperger's syndrome and with a verbal IQ of 153. He found it difficult to cope emotionally and socially with a Rudolf Steiner school, he is mildly apraxic, he has an over-concern with rituals and routines, and spends much of the time in a fantasy world of his own. Despite this, on a battery of linguistic tasks including judgements of grammaticality, tests of inferential ability, the use of discourse connectives, and the construal of discourse referents in ambiguous contexts, KH scored at ceiling. He gave perfect responses to written versions of 'Sally-Anne' (false-belief) tasks; he performed flawlessly on judgements of irony and sarcasm; he correctly identified metaphors, jokes and the use–mention distinction; and he understood a range of examples involving what is known as 'interpretive use' (Sperber and Wilson, 1995) or meta-representational ability of the kind illustrated by the difference between epistemic and deontic modality. He looks like an exception to Happé's (1991:234) remark: 'It is widely reported that even the most verbally able autistic people (that is, people with

Asperger syndrome) fail to understand non-literal speech such as sarcasm, joking and metaphorical expression.'

KH's responses make it unlikely that he has any significant deficit in Theory of Mind, with the obvious implication either that he does not suffer from Asperger's syndrome (despite the un-animous verdict of psychologists and clinicians over several years), or that Asperger's syndrome does not necessarily involve a deficit in Theory of Mind. If the latter conclusion is correct, what are the implications for models of the mind? I think that KH provides evidence for a version of the modularity hypothesis incorporating what Ianthi Tsimpli and I have described as 'quasi-modules' (Tsimpli and Smith, 1998; see also Smith and Tsimpli, 1995). A quasi-module has some of the properties characteristic of Fodorian mod-ules (Fodor, 1983): its operations are domain-specific, mandatory, general to the species, and subject to idiosyncratic pathological breakdown; but more importantly, it does not have **all** of those characteristics: its operations are not informationally encapsulated and the vocabulary over which they operate is conceptual rather than perceptual. We argued that the central system includes a set of (quasi-)modules encompassing at least: (part of) the Language Faculty, Theory of Mind, Moral Judgement, Number, Music, and Social Interaction. KH would then suffer from some deficit in this last quasi-module.

Any account of social interaction needs to include at least categories of 'authority', 'equality' and 'propinquity'. Authority is divided into the 'known' (parents, teachers, etc.) and the 'unknown' (police, traffic wardens, God, etc.). Equality and propinquity are sub-categorized in terms of family versus friends, neighbours and contemporaries, and so on. A host of other vari-ables will also need to be taken into account, including gender, age, sociolinguistic notions of power and solidarity, and on. The details may be undeveloped, but it is clear that KH and other Asperger's subjects lack control of some of these distinctions, treating author-ity figures no differently from friends and family, for instance.

Support for such an analysis comes from recent work by Klin (2000), who has developed a Social Attribution Task and tested it on normal, autistic and Asperger's syndrome subjects. Using geometric shapes that 'act like people' (Klin, 2000:833; cf. Heider and Simmel, 1944), Klin predicted that Asperger's subjects would base their descriptions more on physical/geometric considerations

than social ones. That is, their 'folk physics' should be better pre-
served than their 'folk psychology', where both of these domains
are conceptualized cognitively, lending themselves *prima facie* to quasi-
modular treatment. He claims that a deficit in Theory of Mind alone
is inadequate to explain certain aspects of autistic behaviour, and
that 'having ToM skills does not guarantee commensurate social
adaptation skills' (Klin, 2000:832): in brief, social interaction and
Theory of Mind (doubly) dissociate. Appealing as this account is,
it may be that KH's Theory of Mind is defective, but his elevated
intelligence enables him to compensate linguistically for cognitive
problems of abstract belief, though not for social interaction or emotion. Whatever turns out to be correct, we need an account of the
emotions in which they are independent of general cognition, while
being transparent to social interaction.

The extension of our quasi-modular framework to cover the emotions is less straightforward: emotions are 'level-ubiquitous' in that
one can discuss them physiologically, psychologically or socially, and
it is implausible that the whole gamut should be subserved by one
or even several quasi-modules of the type sufficient (perhaps) to
account for social cognition. However, restricting discussion to the
psychological domain, I will try to indicate how they might interact
with social constructs. Following de Sousa's (1987) ground-breaking
work, I adopt a tri-partite Platonist characterization of human
nature in terms of desire, reason and emotion. Sperber and Wilson
(1995:73–4) have argued for the special status of 'belief' and
'desire' *vis-à-vis* other mental states, and I ascribe a similarly special status to the emotions. That is, these three categories do not
themselves define quasi-modules, but underlie the quasi-modules
that make up the rest of mental structure.

A theory of this domain must meet several conditions. First, it
must not only characterize emotions in the individual, but the individual's identification of emotions in other people. Second, it must
include categories for each of the basic emotions, fear, terror, joy,
happiness, disgust and anger, that are instantly, perhaps univer-
sally, identifiable (see Darwin, 1872; Ekman, 1973, 2004), and are
presumably 'decoded' from physiological evidence: facial expression together with other bodily manifestations such as trembling.
Third, it must provide an account of 'second-order' emotions,
(e.g. shame, embarrassment, envy, jealousy); that is, those whose
identification requires reference to Self and Other, where this

presupposes interaction with both Theory of Mind and Social Judgement, and implies a lack of informational encapsulation. These second-order emotions are inferred on the basis of both visual cues, such as blushing, and other, usually linguistic, evidence; exploiting what is manifestable and hence directly interpretable, as opposed to what is only inferentially computable. Fourth, it must accommodate the fact that even these derived emotions are not of uniform complexity: shame and envy are typically a relation among three entities – two persons and a property: for example, person A envies person B some property or possession C; whereas jealousy is a layered relation among three persons: for example, person A is jealous of person B because of B's relation to person C.

If something of this kind is correct, experiencing derived emotions necessitates the availability of a Theory of Mind, and the identification of derived emotions in others requires both this and some further meta-representational ability. Being shamed or feeling ashamed, for instance, are remarkably complex. There are further refinements that a proper theory will need to incorporate: for instance, the fact that all emotions may be the object of conscious introspection. Gilligan's (2001) moving account of the roots of violence in society starts from the striking observation that violence is frequently a reaction to consciously experienced and expressed feelings of shame.

So where does that leave us with KH and Asperger's syndrome? I think that the condition **may** involve only emotional and social deficits, even if the normal situation is for there to be concomitant deficits in Theory of Mind. So KH, despite his problems, is like Happé's (1991) subject David, who has 'apparently good under-standing of others' minds' (1991:218), but is nonetheless emotionally and socially incomplete. I do not know whether they display 'wonder', but KH and other Asperger's subjects have a character-istic innocence that lets wonder flourish. In his strange and beautiful book Fisher writes (1998:46): 'Those who lack a natural inclination to the passion of wonder are ordinarily very ignorant.' KH is far from ignorant and he certainly rekindles wonder in me.

Acknowledgement

This chapter appeared originally in 2002 in *Glot International* 6:55–7.

Further reading

The case of KH is discussed further in Smith et al. (2003). For recent discussion of autism, see Hill (2004), and especially Frith (2003); and for a 'neural' hypothesis of the emotions, see Gallese et al. (2004).

Glossary

Items marked with a dagger (†) are discussed in the introduction. Items in **bold type** have their own entry in the glossary

accommodation   The phenomenon of speakers modifying their pronunciation (or other aspects of their use of language) to accord more closely with the patterns used by their interlocutors.

adjunct   An optional constituent, frequently an Adverb, which modifies the interpretation of e.g. a Noun Phrase or a Verb Phrase, typically by specifying the time or place of an event or the manner in which the event takes place. Adjuncts are non-arguments.

alethic   That **modality** which conveys truth, as in the use of the modal verb *must* in *He is a bachelor, so he must be unmarried.*

allophone   The allophones of a phoneme are the various different pronunciations it has in different positions in a word. For instance, vowels in English have relatively long allophones before voiced consonants and relatively short allophones before voiceless consonants, so that the phoneme /a/ is pronounced with a longer allophone in *mad* than in *mat.*

ambiguity   The property of having more than one grammatically licensed interpretation, either lexical (e.g. *grave* can mean either 'serious' or 'tomb') or sentential. The sentence *The election was characterized by claims of intimidation by the government* has at least the two interpretations that 'the claims of intimidation were made by the government', and that 'someone claimed that the government used intimidation'. See also **disambiguation**.

analysis-by-synthesis   A model which claims that you analyse an incoming signal by producing a matching version of that signal. For instance, you identify *puzzle* correctly by producing your own version of it. In the example in the text, where the child pronounces *puzzle* like the adult 'puddle', but this latter as 'puggle', any attempt to analyse *puzzle* in terms of his own version would fail.

aphasia   Loss of language as a result of brain damage.

apraxia   Impaired ability to carry out deliberate physical movements.

arbitrariness   See **Saussurean arbitrariness**.

argument   A **constituent** which denotes one of the participants in a situation. In the sentence *Cherie bought a house*, the Noun Phrases *Cherie* and *a house* are arguments of the verb *buy*. In *We hope Cherie bought a house*, the NP *We* and the clause *Cherie bought a house* are arguments of the verb *hope*. The subject *Cherie* is known as the 'external argument' and *a house* is called the 'internal argument'. Arguments are usually Noun Phrases, but not all Noun Phrases are arguments, as some may function as **predicates**.

aspect   A grammatical category whose most salient function is to encode whether the activity described in a sentence is ongoing ('imperfective') or complete ('perfective'), as in the contrast between *He was eating an apple* and *He ate an apple*.

Asperger's syndrome   A form of ('high-functioning') **autism** in which there is no impairment of language or intelligence, but social interaction may still be markedly abnormal.

autism   A developmental disorder resulting in self-absorption, social isolation and often obsessive behaviour. It is standardly attributed to a defect in **Theory of Mind**.

auxiliary   A sub-category of verb, including *can, could, may, might, etc.*, usually used to denote possibility, necessity or ability.

bare plural   A noun used in the plural with no **determiner**, as in *I like cats* (as opposed to *I like the cats*).

†**binding theory**   That part of the theory of grammar which deals with the distribution of anaphors, such as *himself*, and pronouns, such as *him*.

Blimp   A character, Colonel Blimp, invented by the cartoonist David Low, and pictured as a pompous ex-officer voicing a rooted hatred of new ideas.

bound variable   An expression, such as *his (father)* in the sentence *Every boy admires his father*, where the referent varies depending on the choice of individual determined by the quantified **NP** *every boy*.

buffer   See **response buffer**.

†**c-command**   A relation between two nodes in a tree: a node A in a tree c-commands another node B if and only if the first branching node dominating A also dominates B. See the introduction, p. 21, for examples and discussion.

central system   That part of the mind devoted to problem solving and the fixation of belief. It contrasts with the *modules* or input systems which provide some of the information it works on. See also **modularity**.

classifier   A grammatical category found in some languages (Chinese, British Sign Language, etc.) and typically used to specify the kind of noun it precedes in terms of the salient perceived characteristics of the entity to which the associated noun refers. The closest equivalent in English is the use of the underlined nouns in examples such as *two pieces of paper* or *three grains of rice*.

clause   An expression containing a subject and a **predicate**, usually a verb. In *Harold believes that kangaroos can fly* there are two clauses: *kangaroos can fly* and the whole sentence *Harold believes . . .*

cleft   A type of sentence exemplified by *It is dragons that I am obsessed with*, where *dragons* has been **focused**.

code switching   The use of two languages within a single utterance, as in *I suppose cela va sans dire* ('I suppose that goes without saying'), where the speaker has switched from English to French in mid-sentence.

†**competence**   Knowledge of language. See also **I-language**.

complementizer   An item such as *that* which introduces a **clause** which is the complement of a verb like *think* or *believe*, as in *I think that linguistics is fun*.

†**compositionality**   The claim that the meaning of a sentence can be deduced from the meanings of its parts. Idioms (such as *bite the bullet*) are non-compositional.

connectionism   A psychological theory that attempts to reduce thought and other cognitive processes to connections between (models of) brain cells.

consonant harmony   A phonological process, characteristic of the speech of many little children, whereby all the consonants in a word assume the same point of articulation: so *duck* (where the 'd' has an alveolar point of articulation, and the 'ck' a velar point of articulation) might be pronounced (by different children) as either 'guck' or 'dut'.

†**constituent**   In syntax, a group of words that form a structural unit. Technically, a sequence of items that can be traced exhaustively to a single node in a tree.

constraint ranking   In **Optimality Theory** the differences among languages are characterized in terms of how different constraints are ranked (ordered) with respect to each other. For example, the difference between SVO languages like English and SOV languages like Hindi can be captured in terms of whether the constraint HEADRIGHT (the head – here the Verb – must appear on the right) outranks HEADLEFT (the head – here again the Verb – must appear on the left) or vice versa.

context-free   A context-free rule is one which applies in all environments; a context-sensitive one is limited to applying in some environments only. For instance, a child in the early stages of language acquisition might pronounce all consonants as voiced (context-free); somewhat later it might pronounce all consonants as voiced except in final position (context-sensitive).

context-sensitive   See **context-free**.

continuity hypothesis   The claim that all stages in a child's developing grammar represent possible adult grammars. That is, the child's system is not different in kind from the adult system.

contraction   The process whereby a form is reduced to a shortened version, as when *we are* is pronounced *we're*.

control   That part of linguistic theory that deals with relations between Noun Phrases and an understood (empty) category. For example, in *John promised Mary to behave himself*, the empty subject of 'to behave', called **PRO**, is controlled by *John*, because we understand that it is *John's behaving himself* which is intended; in *John told Mary to behave herself*, the empty subject of 'to behave' is controlled by *Mary*, because we understand that it is *Mary's behaving herself* which is intended.

coordination   A process in which two or more items are linked by an element such as *and, or* or *but*, and where both conjuncts have the same syntactic status.

critical period   The period of time during which (e.g.) a child must be exposed to (e.g.) language in order to acquire it perfectly.

default   A form which occurs in the absence of any alternative specification. Plurals in English may be formed in various ways: changing the vowel as in *goose/geese*, adding an irregular suffix as in *ox/oxen*, etc. If no such form is given, the plural is formed, by default, by adding *-s*, as in *cat/cats*, etc.

deontic   The modality (see **modality** (1)) which conveys obligation, as in the use of the modal verb *must* in the example *To vote you must be at least eighteen*. See also **epistemic**.

determiner   Words like *the, this, those, my*, which are used to modify (and **license**) the following noun.

diachronic   Pertaining to development through time, as in historical (or 'diachronic') linguistics. See also **synchronic**.

disambiguation   The **pragmatic** process whereby the intended interpretation of an **ambiguous** sentence is arrived at.

discourse connective   Items like *because, however, nevertheless*, etc. which link sentences in a discourse, giving the hearer guidance in how to construe those sentences appropriately.

dislocation   A syntactic process which moves (dislocates) a **constituent** to the front of the sentence, leaving a pronoun in the original position: for instance, *Hypocrisy, I hate it*.

distinctive features   A set of universal, putatively innate, phonological properties by reference to which it is possible to describe the speech sounds of all possible human languages. Examples include [voiced], [nasal], etc.

distributed system   A system in which (e.g. linguistic) functions are distributed throughout the mind/brain, rather than being strictly localized in one area. It is opposed to some versions of **modularity**.

drift   In historical linguistics, the apparent trend for language change to take a particular direction so that the language ends up with a consistent set of properties.

easy-to-please **construction**   See *tough*-**movement**.

echo-question   A question which seeks information about a misheard or disbelieved part of a preceding utterance by repeating everything except that part: *You saw <u>who</u> dancing with Harry?*

†**E-language**   Human language viewed not as a psychological construct, but as a set of sentences existing in the public domain, independently of (*external* to) particular individuals. See also **I-language**.

embedded   A clause or other constituent included within the structure of a larger sentence is said to be embedded in that sentence. In *Deirdre thinks that ducks are mammals*, the sequence *that ducks are mammals* is embedded as the complement of the verb *think*.

†**empty category**   A grammatical category which has syntactic and semantic properties but is not pronounced; as the understood subject 'you' in *Leave me alone*; or the PRO (see **control**) subject of *elope* in *John wants to elope*.

encode   To relate a semantic or conceptual category systematically to some definable grammatical form. Plurality is encoded in the grammar of English but not in the grammar of Chinese.

epistemic   The modality (see **modality** (1)) which conveys belief, as in the use of the modal verb *must* in the example *To own all those cars you must be awfully rich*. See also **deontic**.

evaluation measure   An algorithm for choosing among alternative grammars, all of which seem at first sight to be equally successful. One such device was postulated in early generative grammar as an account of first language acquisition, but was largely superseded by the alternative claims of the **Principles and Parameters** framework.

event time See **reference time**.

evidential(ity) A grammatical category used to indicate the source of the information expressed: as hearsay, inference or eye-witness account, for example. The subjunctive mood often serves this purpose in, for instance, German, where *er ist krank* asserts as a fact that 'He is ill', whereas *er sei krank* (where *sei* is the subjunctive form of 'to be') intimates that 'He is or may be, or is rumoured to be ill', but the speaker is not able to confirm the validity of the claim.

existential quantifier See **quantifier**.

external argument See **argument**.

extraction Another term for **movement**, emphasizing the source of the item moved – for example, from inside a **clause** or a Noun Phrase.

facial action A component of signed languages such as British Sign Language in which particular facial configurations, such as furrowed eyebrows, encode specific linguistic meanings.

faithfulness In **Optimality Theory**, a class of constraints which favour forms which deviate minimally from (are 'faithful' to) some input.

false belief The ability, which develops at about four years of age, to understand that other people can have views which differ from your own or from reality. The ability is central to the **Theory of Mind**, and is characteristically lacking in **autistic** subjects.

†falsifiability A fundamental requirement of any scientific enterprise is that its hypotheses be testable, that is, falsifiable in principle. A simplistic form of this requirement, known as 'naive falsificationism', would reject a theory any of whose hypotheses was falsified. Rational scientists attempt to preserve what is good in such a theory by modifying some of its claims.

falsificationism See **falsifiability**.

feature geometry A part of the theory of phonology which associates particular sets of features by linking them in a geometrical display, to account for the fact that they operate together systematically in (e.g.) the process of assimilation whereby the 'n' in *ten* is pronounced as an [m] before the 'p' in *ten people*.

feedback loop   A device which sends information about the output of some action or process to the input stage of that action or process.

filler-gap   A construction in which some item has been moved and the position vacated is filled by a **trace**: as in *Which penguin$_i$ did you see t$_i$ in the igloo?*

finite   A finite **clause** is one containing a finite verb or auxiliary: that is, one which allows a choice of tense, as in the contrast between *they eat caterpillars* and *they ate caterpillars*. Non-finite clauses include participles and infinitives.

focus   A grammatical process, either syntactic or phonological, which highlights a particular **constituent**, typically in answer to a question. The item *bats* is focused in each of the answers to the question 'What did Mary write a book about?' Answer 1: 'She wrote a book about **bats**' (with stress on 'bats'); Answer 2: '**Bats**, Mary wrote a book about'.

†**functional category**   A category which includes **determiners**, tense, **complementizers** and (some) prepositions, etc. and excludes Nouns, Verbs and Adjectives. Functional categories and their properties are the major source of differences among the languages of the world. See also **lexical category**.

†**generative (grammar)**   A grammar is generative if it uses an explicit set of formal rules and principles to characterize ('generate') the sentences or other **constituent**s of a language.

geometry   See **feature geometry**.

glide   An articulation produced in the transition from one sound to another; for instance, the 'y' ([j]) sound between the [b] and the [u:] in *beauty*.

Government (and Binding)   A stage of generative grammar, encapsulated in Chomsky (1981), in which two of the central notions were 'government' in something like its traditional grammatical usage, and **binding**.

GPSG (Generalized Phrase Structure Grammar)   A theory of grammar, encapsulated in Gazdar et al. (1985), which eschewed transformations in favour of an extended system of Phrase Structure rules.

grammaticality The property of a sentence of conforming to the rules and principles of an explicit grammar. It is one of the factors which determine whether a sentence when uttered is acceptable. Sentences may manifest degrees of grammaticality.

HPSG (Head-driven Phrase Structure Grammar) A constraint-based, lexicalist approach to grammatical theory, which originated as an extension of **GPSG**.

iconicity Resemblance between the meaning of a linguistic expression and its sound (onomatopoeia) or sign. For instance, the sign in British Sign Language for a telephone is a handshape imitative of an old-fashioned telephone. See also **Saussurean arbitrariness**.

idiolect The **I-language** of an individual.

†I-language Knowledge of language. Language viewed as a construct *i*nternal to the mind of the *i*ndividual. The technical term for **competence**. See also **E-language**.

imaging Any of a variety of techniques for monitoring the activity of the brain. The best known are **fMRI** (functional Magnetic Resonance Imaging), **PET scan** (Positron Emission Tomography) and **ERP** (Event-Related Potential).

imperfect The form of the verb exemplified in *She was eating an apple*. In English the main interpretation of the imperfect is as 'imperfective'. See **aspect**.

implicature In pragmatics, an assumption which is communicated, but not explicitly communicated. The utterance *You're on a diet* has a possible implicature that the addressee should not eat another bun.

incorporation A syntactic process, characteristic especially of some **polysynthetic** languages, whereby a noun is incorporated into the structure of a verb: for instance, *to housekeep*.

inference That stage in the interpretation of utterances which relies on logical processes outside the grammar (i.e. in the central system). Given an utterance such as *It's nearly dead*, you decode the message that some entity is close to death, and then infer that the 'it' refers to the family pet, that you should call the vet, or tell your spouse not to exaggerate, etc.

informational encapsulation   The claim, made famous by Jerry Fodor (1983), that the internal workings of **modules** (such as vision, hearing and language) are not sensitive to knowledge from the **central system**. So knowing that a visual illusion *is* an illusion doesn't stop your (encapsulated) visual system from seeing it *as* an illusion.

intensional   Related to the meaning of a concept rather than its referent. The expressions *Morning Star* and *Evening Star* have the same referent (Venus) but different intensions.

internal argument   See **argument**.

interpretive use   The use of an utterance to represent some state of affairs indirectly as an 'interpretation' of a thought of someone other than the speaker. The ironical use of *He's a genius* is interpretive in this sense.

†**intuitions**   Judgements of well-formedness or ill-formedness that native speakers are able to make about sentences of their language. They do not have comparably valid intuitions about the appropriate analysis of those sentences.

invited inference   A conclusion you are led to make without it being logically valid. For instance, if I offer you £10 to mow my lawn, you are tacitly invited to infer that I will not give you £10 if you do not mow my lawn.

island (effect)   The effect (on e.g. **extraction**) of a particular syntactic configuration. For instance, *John said that rabbits eat carrots* can be questioned to give: *What did John say [that rabbits eat]?*, but *That rabbits eat carrots distresses her* does not allow the question *What does [that rabbits eat] distress her?*, because in the latter sentence the *carrots* are part of the subject of the sentence, and subjects are islands.

language of thought (LoT)   That system with which we think and carry out inferencing.

†**level of representation**   Our linguistic knowledge is of various different kinds: phonological, syntactic, and so on. Each of the components of the grammar dealing with these different kinds of knowledge defines a level of representation. Much of the history of modern linguistics has revolved around the attempt to answer

questions about the number and nature of the levels it is necessary to postulate.

lexical category   One of the categories Noun, Verb, Adjective and (perhaps) Preposition which have substantive content. They are in contrast with **functional categories**.

lexical entry   Every item of vocabulary we know must feature in the mental lexicon. This consists of a set of lexical entries, each of which specifies the properties of the item concerned: for example, that *penguin* is a Noun, begins with a 'p', refers to a kind of flightless bird, and so on.

LF (Logical Form)   A **level of representation** in the grammar which encodes the meanings of the sentences involved, and constitutes an interface with the conceptual system.

LF' (Logical Form prime)   A putative **level of representation** outside the language faculty proper, and which constitutes a bridge between **LF** and the **language of thought**.

licensing   The requirement that linguistic entities need to satisfy some condition in order to constitute part of a well-formed sentence – they need to be licensed. The simplest form of the phenomenon occurs with 'case' licensing. In German, for example, different verbs license different cases, so that *sehen* (to see) must be followed by an accusative, as in *Ich sehe ihn* (I see him), whereas *helfen* (to help) must be followed by a dative, as in *Ich helfe ihm* (I help him).

markedness   Part of the theory of language which attempts to account for the relative probability of alternative forms or interpretations: the more common form is then said to be unmarked, the less likely is marked. For instance, *duck* has the unmarked interpretation of denoting any member of the Anatidae, and a marked interpretation of denoting only the female, where the male is a *drake*. In **Optimality Theory** the different ranking of markedness constraints and faithfulness constraints jointly accounts for the possible differences among languages. See also **default**.

maven   A humorous and slightly sardonic term for an expert.

mean length of utterance (MLU)   In first language acquisition the child's current stage of development is often computed in terms of the average length, in terms of words or **morphemes**, of the sentences it utters.

metalinguistic   Pertaining to the use of language to describe language.

minimal pair   A pair of items which illustrate a maximally simple contrast, such as the phonological difference between *illusion* and *allusion*; or the syntactic difference between *John is easy to please* and *John is eager to please*.

modality (1)   A conceptual category embodying possibility, necessity, or the opinion and attitude of the speaker. It is conveyed (in English) by 'modal' verbs such as *can, might, must*.

modality (2)   The channel of communication – signed or spoken.

modularity   The claim that cognition is compartmentalized such that the mind consists of a set of modules (such as vision, language, number, music, moral judgement), each of which is in part independent of the others, can operate autonomously, and can break down idiosyncratically. Views on modularity are extremely diverse and all of them are controversial. See also **distributed system, neural network**.

module   See **modularity**.

morpheme   The minimal syntactic unit. Words consist of morphemes, so 'lionesses' consists of the three morphemes {lion}, {-ess} and {-es}, of which the first happens also to be a word, but the latter two can occur only in conjunction with such a word. Morphemes are conventionally put in {curly brackets}.

morphologization   The process (**synchronic** or **diachronic**) whereby a syntactic or semantic category becomes **encoded** in the (morphological) structure of a word.

†**morphology**   That part of linguistic theory which deals with the internal structure of words. For instance, the word *transformations* is composed of the elements *transform, -ation*, and *-s*; and even *transform* can be broken down into *trans* and *form*.

motherese   A form of language used when talking to or about young children, involving the use of forms such as 'bunny', 'doggie', and putative simplifications to the grammar. Baby-talk.

movement   The displacement of some item from the position where it is understood. In *John was kissed by a mermaid* and *She kissed John passionately*, the item *John* is interpreted in much the same way in both sentences: that is, as undergoing an act of kissing. It is said to have moved to the front of the sentence in the first of the examples. See also **transformation, trace**.

neural network   A device consisting of a set of processing units arranged in a network which is supposed to simulate the neural structure of the brain. It is frequently invoked as an implementation of, or an alternative to, symbolic models. See also **connectionism, modularity**.

non-finite   See **finite**.

NP (Noun Phrase)   A phrase with a noun as its head, exemplified by such constituents as *John, the penguin, all my friends*, etc.

OED   The *Oxford English Dictionary*.

offglide   The second element of a complex sound, such as a cluster or a diphthong, exemplified by the two underlined elements in *tro̲u̲sers* ([tra̲u̲zəz]). See also **glide**.

operator   A function whose output is of the same kind as its input. For instance, the negative operator may take a (positive) verb phrase as its input and give a (negative) verb phrase as its output.

Optimality Theory (OT)   A conception of grammar in which 'optimality' with respect to a set of constraints defines well-formedness. That form is optimal which violates the fewest, or the least highly ranked, constraints. See also **constraint ranking**.

OV (Object Verb)   A common locus of difference among languages is the relative order of the Verb and its direct Object. Languages like Hindi or Japanese, in which the object precedes the verb, are known as OV languages. Languages like English, in which the verb precedes the object, are known as VO languages.

parameter   See **Principles and Parameters**.

parasitic gap   A construction, exemplified by *This is the book that I reviewed * without reading **, which contains two **empty categories** (indicated by the asterisks), the second of which is said to be parasitic on the first.

particle   An informal term used to describe elements that don't fit neatly into the list of parts of speech. It includes examples like *to*, in *to* love, and *up*, in *eat up your dinner*.

†performance   The use of one's knowledge of language to produce and understand sentences and to give judgements of ambiguity, well-formedness, etc. See also **competence**.

†phonetics   That part of the theory of language that deals with sounds, especially sounds viewed as physical phenomena rather than as elements in a (phonological) system.

†phonology   That part of linguistic theory that deals with the sound systems and sound structures of **I-language**.

pleiotropy   In genetics, the production by a single gene of two or more apparently unrelated phenotypic effects.

polarity items   Words such as *ever* and *any* that need to be **licensed** by a preceding negative (or question, etc.). Thus, it is possible to say *Has he ever been there?* and *He hasn't ever been there*; but it is ungrammatical to say *He has ever been there*.

polysynthetic   A kind of language, such as Inuit or Navajo, characterized by extremely complex **morphology**.

PP   See **Prepositional Phrase**.

†pragmatics   The study of the interpretation of utterances. It presupposes a linguistic analysis of the sentences to which those utterances correspond.

predicate   The property attributed to the subject of a sentence by the rest of the sentence. In *The puppy is a nuisance* the property of 'being a nuisance' is predicated of 'the puppy'.

Prepositional Phrase   A phrase, such as *in the garden*, which is headed by a preposition.

priming   A psychological technique in which the speed of response to a particular stimulus is increased by 'priming' the subject with a related word. For instance, if you are asked to press a key on the computer as soon as you see the word *queen*, you will react faster if you have just seen *king* than if you have just seen *ink*, or have had no previous input. *King* is then said to 'prime' *queen*.

†**Principles and Parameters** A major theory in current generative linguistics. Linguistic theory is said to consist of a set of universal *principles*, such as the principle of **structure dependence**, and a number of *parameters*, whose settings characterize the differences among languages, such as whether they are *pro*-**drop** or not. In recent versions of the theory, parameters are restricted to properties of **functional categories**. First language acquisition consists in large part of the child 'setting the parameters' of the language or languages to which he or she is exposed.

PRO The invisible subject of a **non-finite** clause of the kind exemplified in *Carlos wants [PRO to be a saint]*. See also **control**.

pro-**drop** The property, characteristic of Spanish, Greek and many other languages, of allowing subject pronouns to be omitted in finite clauses. In Spanish, one can say either *ella baila bien* ('she dances well') or *baila bien* ('dances well'), whereas in English only the former is possible as a complete sentence.

pro-form An item such as a pronoun which may replace a full Noun Phrase, as in *The penguin ate a fish and then it waddled away*, where *it* is a pro-form for *the penguin*. Most syntactic categories have their respective pro-forms, so a VP may be replaced by the pro-form *do so* in examples like: *Most rabbits reproduce rapidly and most gerbils do so too*, where *do so* is a pro-form for the VP *reproduce rapidly*.

proposition The semantic content of a declarative sentence when uttered by a particular person on a particular occasion. The sentence *Esme loves me* may be true or false when uttered by different people, or by the same person on different occasions.

quantifier Any element, such as *all, some, few, 23, most*, etc. which indicate the quantity of the associated noun in a Noun Phrase. *All* is known as the universal quantifier, and *some* as the existential quantifier.

quasi-module A component of the mind that has some of the properties of **modules** (input systems), but which operates on a conceptual rather than a perceptual vocabulary and is not **informationally encapsulated**.

†**recursion** The property of language whereby one phrase can be **embedded** inside another without limit, giving rise to the infinite expressive power of all human languages.

reductionism   The attempt to explain the generalizations of one science in terms of another, more basic, science; ultimately always physics. For instance, some writers attempt to reduce knowledge of language to neurology.

reference time   A point in time distinct from both the time of utterance (speech time) and the time of the event described in the sentence uttered (event time). In *He had eaten the pie (before I arrived)*, the event of pie-eating took place not only before speech time but also before the reference time established either in the sentence or in the context. In the example given, the reference time is given by *before I arrived*.

relativism   The view that languages, cultures and other social constructs may vary without limit. It is in contrast to universalist views under which *all* languages (and cultures) share particular properties.

repair   Self-correction by a speaker, as illustrated in: *I saw a liz . . . I mean a snake*.

response buffer   A temporary store into which information is transferred while awaiting the action of some other component of the system.

Sally-Anne   A psychological test of so-called **false belief**. While the subject (Sally) and an observer (Anne) are both watching, the experimenter 'hides' an object – for instance, a key – in position X. Anne is then sent out of the room and the key is removed to a different position Y. Sally is now asked where Anne will look for the key when she returns. Older children and adults answer X; children below the age of four (and **autistic** subjects) typically reply 'Y'. The standard interpretation is that they are unable to formulate 'false beliefs' or, more plausibly, that they are unable consciously to reflect on such beliefs. See also **Smarties**.

Saussurean arbitrariness   The arbitrary relation between the sound and meaning of a word. That is, there is no inherent relation between the sound of the word *pig* and the meaning of that word. Marginal exceptions are provided by onomatopoeia and iconic signs. See also **iconicity**.

schwa   The name for the neutral vowel [ə] heard in English at the beginning of words such as *'above'*.

†scope The scope of an expression is the set of items which fall within its sphere of influence. For instance, in the apparently parallel sentences *She couldn't eat the melon* and *She shouldn't eat the melon*, the scope of negation may be different. The former can be paraphrased as *It is not the case that she could eat the melon* (with *could* in the scope of *not*); the latter can be paraphrased as *It is the case that she should not eat the melon* (with *not* in the scope of *should*).

†semantics The study of meaning.

sensori-motor Pertaining to the physiological apparatus responsible for our ability to produce and perceive (e.g.) sentences.

sequence of tense In some contexts the choice of tense, past or present, is inhibited by a rule of sequence of tense. For instance, if *Susan is ill* and we have been informed of this by Tom, we can report the situation with the sentence *Tom said that Susan was ill*. The choice of *was* is forced on us (or at least many speakers) by the past tense of the preceding verb *said*.

slash category A category with an element missing. In *This is the book we believe John read*, the sequence 'John read' is a sentence with a missing Noun Phrase (actually 'the book' which shows up earlier). Such categories, invented by Gerald Gazdar as an alternative to using transformations, are standardly written with a slash preceding the missing element; in this case 'S/NP'.

Smarties A psychological test in which participants are shown a Smarties tube (a tube containing chocolate sweets; the American equivalent is M&M) and asked what they think is in it. After answering 'Smarties', they are shown that it really contains (e.g.) a pencil. They are then asked what they predict that a friend will think is in it. Children below the age of four or so, and **autistic** subjects, typically reply 'a pencil', suggesting that they are unable to formulate **false beliefs** or, more plausibly, that they are unable consciously to reflect on such beliefs. See also **Sally-Anne**.

Specific Language Impairment (SLI) A developmental disorder in which sufferers show normal intelligence, have no obvious other disabilities, but manifest serious difficulties in their knowledge and use of language.

speech time See **reference time**.

†**structure-dependence**   All syntactic rules in all languages operate on structures rather than on unstructured strings of words. For example, to form a question in English one moves the auxiliary to the left of the subject Noun Phrase, deriving, for example, *Has the postman been?* from *The postman has been*. It is not possible for any human language to have a rule that moves 'the third word from the left', or that permutes the second and fifth words. In brief, rules of grammar cannot count.

synchronic   Pertaining to (the study of) language at a single point in time, as opposed to historically. See also **diachronic**.

†**syntax**   The branch of linguistics that deals with the arrangement of words in a sentence.

TEFL   Teaching of English as a Foreign Language.

template   A fixed pattern adopted by a child acquiring its first language, whereby (e.g.) all words of more than one syllable might adopt the same form. For example, all words with non-initial stress might be pronounced with *re-* as the first syllable.

TESL   Teaching of English as a Second Language.

that-**trace**   A syntactic constraint which prohibits the occurrence of *that* next to a **trace** (an **empty category**). It accounts for the contrasting acceptability in English of such examples as *Who do you think came?* and the ungrammatical *Who do you think that came?*

thematic relation/theta role   The semantic role associated with the **argument**s of a verb. For example, *walk* requires a Noun Phrase with the role of 'agent', *kiss* requires Noun Phrases with the roles of 'agent' and 'patient'.

Theory of Mind (ToM)   A **module** of the mind that allows us to entertain the possibility that other people have minds just as we do. It enables us to infer what others are thinking in order to explain and predict their behaviour. It might more accurately be called a Theory of Other Minds.

topicalization   A syntactic process which highlights the entity that the sentence is about, typically by moving it to the front of the sentence. In *Linguistics, this book is about*, the word *Linguistics* has been topicalized. See also **focus**.

tough-**movement**   A syntactic process that relates sentences such as *Gladys is hard/tough to talk to* to its putative source, *It is hard/tough to talk to Gladys*, by moving *Gladys* from object to subject position. Also known as the *easy-to-please* construction.

trace   An **empty category** marking the place from which a constituent has been **moved**.

†**transformation**   A grammatical rule which converts one structure into another by moving some **constituent**. In earlier versions of **generative grammar**, transformations converted 'deep structures' into 'surface structures'.

trigger   Linguistic data which enable a child to set a particular **parametric** choice. For instance, hearing *drink your milk* (with the verb preceding the object) may be sufficient to let the child decide that it is learning a **VO** language rather than an **OV** language.

type   The semantic category associated with particular syntactic constructs. For instance, the (internal) argument of a verb may have the type either of an individual (as in *Fred ate the duckling*) or of a proposition (as in *Fred thought the duckling was tasty*).

UG (Universal Grammar)   The innate endowment that the new-born child brings to the task of acquiring its first language. It consists of a set of principles and a number of parameters that the child fixes on the basis of exposure to incoming linguistic stimuli. See also **Principles and Parameters**.

underspecification   If not all the information is given in (e.g.) a **lexical entry**, it is said to be underspecified. For instance, the content of unstressed syllables may be left vague or underspecified in early stages of language acquisition. Similarly, the intended interpretation of sentences is usually only hinted at by their linguistic form, leaving the details to be filled in (or not) by the hearer: for example, *I'm too tired* leaves vague the nature of my tiredness.

universal quantifier   See **quantifier**.

unmarked   See **marked**.

use/mention   In a sentence like *Dragons are frightening*, the word *dragons* is being used; in the **metalinguistic** sentence *'Dragons' has* *seven letters*, it is being mentioned, as indicated by the inverted commas and the use of *has* rather than *have*.

V-bar   A **constituent** intermediate in size between a lexical verb and a full Verb Phrase. Current theories try to do without it.

velar   Any speech sound articulated with contact between the velum and the back of the tongue: e.g. 'k', 'g', and 'ng' ([ŋ]) in English.

verb-second (V2)   A syntactic rule which moves the verb into second position in the **clause**, and an informal typological designation for languages such as German in which such movement is obligatory in main clauses.

V O (Verb Object)   See **OV**.

VP (Verb Phrase)   A phrase with a verb as its head, exemplified by such constituents as *eat a haddock*, *play with the children*, *think that it is cold*, etc.

V to I movement   A syntactic rule which moves a verb from its original position under V to be immediately dominated by I (the head of the Inflection Phrase). In English, it accounts for the **movement** of the auxiliary verb *have* in *Have you seen the Wombles?* In many languages, including earlier stages of English, this movement could apply to main verbs as well, hence the Shakespearean *Knows he not thy voice?*

Wh-word   A word, such as *who, what, which, whether*, used to introduce questions requiring specific information.

References

Acredolo, L. (2000) Letter in INFO-CHILDES, dated 29 March.

Acredolo, L. and S. Goodwyn (1988) 'Symbolic gesturing in normal infants'. *Child Development* 59:450–66.

Acredolo, L. and S. Goodwyn (1996) *Baby Signs: How to Talk With Your Baby Before Your Baby Can Talk*. Chicago, Contemporary Books.

Adger, D. (2003) *Core Syntax: A Minimalist Approach*. Oxford, Oxford University Press.

Anderson, D. (2002) 'Structural ambiguity in early English *tough* constructions: Are child grammars deficient or simply different from adult grammars?'. *Working Papers in English and Applied Linguistics*. RCEAL, University of Cambridge 8:1–24.

Anderson, S. (2004) *Doctor Dolittle's Delusion*. New Haven, CT, Yale University Press.

Baddeley, A. (2003) 'Working memory and language: An overview'. *Journal of Communication Disorders* 36:189–208.

Baillargeon, R. (1995) 'Physical reasoning in infancy'. In M. Gazzaniga (ed.) *The Cognitive Neurosciences*. Cambridge, MA, MIT Press, pp. 181–204.

Baillargeon, R., E. Spelke and S. Wasserman (1985) 'Object permanence in five-month-old infants'. *Cognition* 20:191–208.

Baker, M. (2001a) 'The natures of nonconfigurationality'. In M. Baltin and C. Collins (eds.) *The Handbook of Contemporary Syntactic Theory*. Oxford, Blackwell, pp. 407–38.

Baker, M. (2001b) *The Atoms of Language: The Mind's Hidden Rules of Grammar*. Oxford, Oxford University Press.

Baker, M. (2003) 'Linguistic differences and language design'. *Trends in Cognitive Sciences* 7:349–53.

Bakrick, L., D. Netto and M. Hernandez-Reif (1998) 'Intermodal perception of adult and child faces and voices by infants'. *Child Development* 69:1263–75.

Baltin, M. (2001) 'A-Movements'. In M. Baltin and C. Collins (eds.) *The Handbook of Contemporary Syntactic Theory*. Oxford, Blackwell, pp. 226–54.

Baron-Cohen, S. (1995) *Mindblindness: An Essay on Autism and Theory of Mind*. Cambridge, MA, MIT Press.

Bates, E. and J. Elman (1996) 'Learning rediscovered'. *Science* 274:1849–50.

Bauby, J.-D. (1997) *The Diving-Bell and the Butterfly*. London, Fourth Estate.

Bloom, P. (2000) *How Children Learn the Meanings of Words*. Cambridge, MA, MIT Press.

Bloomfield, L. (1935) *Language*. London, Allen and Unwin.

Boghossian, P. (1996) 'What the Sokal Hoax ought to teach us: the pernicious consequences and internal contradictions of "postmodernist" relativism'. *Times Literary Supplement* (13 December).

Borer, H. and K. Wexler (1987) 'The maturation of syntax'. In T. Roeper and E. Williams (eds.) *Parameter Setting*. Dordrecht, Reidel; pp. 123–72.

Bowerman, M. and S. Levinson (eds.) (2001) *Language Acquisition and Conceptual Development*. Cambridge, Cambridge University Press.

Bowers, J. (2001) 'Predication'. In M. Baltin and C. Collins (eds.) *The Handbook of Contemporary Syntactic Theory*. Oxford, Blackwell, pp. 299–333.

Braine, M. (1971) 'On two models of the internalisation of grammars'. In D. Slobin (ed.) *The Ontogenesis of Grammar*. New York, Academic Press pp. 153–86.

Brien, D. (ed.) (1992) *Dictionary of British Sign Language/English*. London, Faber and Faber.

Briscoe, T. (ed.) (2002) *Linguistic Evolution through Language Acquisition*. Cambridge, Cambridge University Press.

Brodsky, J. (1987) 'On "September 1, 1939" by W. H. Auden'. In *Less than One: Selected Essays*. Harmondsworth, Penguin, pp. 304–56.

Brody, M. and R. Manzini (1988) 'On implicit arguments'. In R. Kempson (ed.) *Mental Representations: The Interface between language and Reality*. Cambridge, Cambridge University Press, pp. 105–30.

Brown, E. K. (ed.) (in prep.) *Encyclopedia of Language and Linguistics*. Elsevier.

Brown, G. (1995) *Speakers, Listeners, and Communication: Explorations in Discourse Analysis*. Cambridge, Cambridge University Press.

Brown, R. (1973) *A First Language: The Early Stages*. Harmondsworth, Penguin.

Butterworth, B. (1999) *The Mathematical Brain*. London, Macmillan.

Caramazza, A. and K. Shapiro (2004) 'Language categories in the brain: evidence from aphasia'. In A. Belletti (ed.) *Structures and Beyond: The*

Cartography of Syntactic Structures. Vol. 3. Oxford, Oxford University Press, pp. 15–38.

Carston, R. (2002) *Thoughts and Utterances: The Pragmatics of Explicit Communication.* Oxford, Blackwell.

Chierchia, G. (1998) 'Reference to kinds across languages' *Natural Language Semantics* 6:339–405.

Chierchia, G. and S. McConnell-Ginet (2000) *Meaning and Grammar: An Introduction to Semantics.* 2nd edn. Cambridge MA, MIT Press.

Chomsky, C. (1986) 'Analytic study of the Tadoma method: language abilities of three deaf–blind subjects'. *Journal of Speech and Hearing Research* 29:332–47.

Chomsky, N. (1957) *Syntactic Structures.* The Hague, Mouton.

Chomsky, N. (1959) Review of Skinner, 1957. *Language* 35:26–58. [Reprinted in J. Fodor and J. Katz (eds.) (1964) *The Structure of Language: Readings in the Philosophy of Language*: Englewood Cliffs, NJ, Prentice-Hall, pp. 547–78.]

Chomsky, N. (1965) *Aspects of the Theory of Syntax.* Cambridge, MA, MIT Press.

Chomsky, N. (1975) *Reflections on Language.* New York, Pantheon.

Chomsky, N. (1980a) *Rules and Representations.* Oxford, Blackwell.

Chomsky, N. (1980b) 'On binding'. *Linguistic Inquiry* 11:1–46.

Chomsky, N. (1980c) 'The new organology'. *Behavioral and Brain Sciences* 3:42–61.

Chomsky, N. (1981) *Lectures on Government and Binding.* Dordrecht, Foris.

Chomsky, N. (1984) *Modular Approaches to the Study of Mind.* San Diego, San Diego State University Press.

Chomsky, N. (1994) 'Chomsky, Noam'. In S. Guttenplan (ed.) *A Companion to the Philosophy of Mind.* Oxford, Blackwell, pp. 153–67.

Chomsky, N. (1995a) *The Minimalist Program.* Cambridge, MA, MIT Press.

Chomsky, N. (1995b) 'Language and nature'. *Mind* 104:1–61.

Chomsky, N. (2000a) *New Horizons in the Study of Language and Mind.* Cambridge, Cambridge University Press.

Chomsky, N. (2000b) 'Minimalist inquiries: the framework'. In R. Martin, D. Michaels and J. Uriagereka (eds.) *Step by Step: Essays on Minimalist Syntax in Honor of Howard Lasnik.* Cambridge, MA, MIT Press, pp. 89–155.

Chomsky, N. (2001) *Propaganda and the Public Mind.* London, Pluto Press.

Chomsky, N. (2002a) *On Nature and Language.* Cambridge, Cambridge University Press.

Chomsky, N. (2002b) *Understanding Power: The Indispensable Chomsky.* Eds P. Mitchell and J. Schoeffel. New York, New Press. [Explanatory footnotes available at www.understandingpower.com.]

Chomsky, N. (2003) 'Replies'. In L. Antony and N. Hornstein (eds.) *Chomsky and his Critics.* Oxford, Blackwell, pp. 255–328.

Chomsky, N. (2004) 'Beyond explanatory adequacy'. In A. Belletti (ed.) *Structures and Beyond: The Cartography of Syntactic Structures. Vol. 3*. Oxford, Oxford University Press, pp. 104–31.

Chomsky, N. and E. Herman (1979) *The Political Economy of Human Rights. Vol. 1: The Washington Connection and Third World Fascism*. Nottingham, Spokesman.

Chomsky, W. (1957) *Hebrew: The Eternal Language*. Philadelphia, Jewish Publication Society of America.

Christiansen, M. and S. Kirby (2003) 'Language evolution: consensus and controversies'. *Trends in Cognitive Sciences* 7:300–7.

Clark, E. (2001) 'Emergent categories in first language acquisition'. In M. Bowerman and S. Levinson (eds.) *Language Acquisition and Conceptual Development*. Cambridge, Cambridge University Press, pp. 379–405.

Clark, E. (2003) *First Language Acquisition*. Cambridge, Cambridge University Press.

Clark, E. (2004) 'How language acquisition builds on cognitive development'. *Trends in Cognitive Sciences* 8:472–8.

Collins, J. (2004) 'Faculty disputes'. *Mind & Language* 19:503–33.

Comrie, B. (1985) *Tense*. Cambridge, Cambridge University Press.

Comrie, B. (1986) 'Tense in indirect speech'. *Folia Linguistica* 20:265–96.

Cooper, R. (1982) 'Binding in wholewheat* syntax (*unenriched with inaudibilia)'. In P. Jacobson and G. K. Pullum (eds.) *The Nature of Syntactic Representation*. Dordrecht, Reidel, pp. 59–78.

Corballis, M. (2004) 'FOXP2 and the mirror system'. *Trends in Cognitive Sciences* 8:95–6.

Cormack, A. and I. Roberts (2004) 'Bound variable pronouns and agreement features'. Paper presented to the LAGB, University of Surrey, Roehampton, August.

Cormack, A. and N. V. Smith (2002) 'Modals and negation in English'. In S. Barbiers, F. Beukema and W. van der Wurff (eds.) *Modality and its Interaction with the Verbal System*. Amsterdam, John Benjamins, pp. 133–63.

Cowart, W. (1997) *Experimental Syntax: Applying Objective Methods to Sentence Judgments*. London, Sage.

Crain, S. and P. Pietroski (2002) 'Why language acquisition is a snap'. *Linguistic Review* 19:163–83.

Creider, C. and R. Hudson (2002) 'Case agreement in ancient Greek: implications for a theory of covert elements'. ftp://ftp.phon.ucl.ac.uk/pub/Word-Grammar/greek.pdf.

Crystal, D. (1988) *The English Language*. London, Penguin.

Crystal, D. (2000) *Language Death*. Cambridge, Cambridge University Press.

Culicover, P. (1999) *Syntactic Nuts: Hard Cases, Syntactic Theory and Language Acquisition*. Oxford, Oxford University Press.

Darwin, C. (1872) *The Expression of Emotion in Man and Animals*. London, John Murray.

Davies, L. (2002) 'Specific language impairment as principle conflict: evidence from negation'. *Lingua* 112:281–300.

Declerck, R. (1991) *Tense in English: Its Structure and Use in Discourse*. London, Routledge.

Dehaene, S. (1997) *The Number Sense*. London, Allen Lane.

De Sousa, R. (1987) *The Rationality of Emotion*. Cambridge, MA, MIT Press.

De Villiers, J. and P. de Villiers (2000) 'Linguistic determinism and the understanding of false beliefs'. In P. Mitchell and K. Riggs (eds.) *Children's Reasoning and the Mind*. New York, Psychology Press, pp. 189–226.

De Witt, H. (2000) *The Last Samurai*. London, Vintage.

Dinnsen, D. (1992) 'Variation in developing and fully developed phonetic inventories'. In C. Ferguson, L. Menn and C. Stoel-Gammon (eds.) *Phonological Development: Models, Research, Implications*. Timonium, MD, York Press, pp. 191–210.

Ekman, P. (1973) *Darwin and Facial Expression: A Century of Research in Review*. New York, Academic Press.

Ekman, P. (2004) 'Happy, sad, angry, disgusted'. In 'Secrets of the Face': *New Scientist* (2 October), 4–5.

Elman, J. (2004) 'An alternative view of the mental lexicon'. *Trends in Cognitive Sciences* 8:301–6.

Enard, W., M. Przeworski, S. Fisher, C. Lai, V. Wiebe, T. Kitano, A. Monaco and S. Pääbo (2002) 'Molecular evolution of FOXP2, a gene involved in speech and language'. *Nature* 418:869–72.

Fabb, N. (2002) *Language and Literary Structure: The Linguistic Analysis of Form in Verse and Narrative*. Cambridge, Cambridge University Press.

Feigenson, L., S. Dehaene and E. Spelke (2004) 'Core systems of number'. *Trends in Cognitive Sciences* 8:307–14.

Ferguson, C., L. Menn and C. Stoel-Gammon (eds.) (1992) *Phonological Development: Models, Research, Implications*. Timonium, MD, York Press.

Fisher, P. (1998) *Wonder, the Rainbow and the Aesthetics of Rare Experiences*. Cambridge, MA, Harvard University Press.

Fodor, J. (1975) *The Language of Thought*. New York, Crowell.

Fodor, J. (1983) *The Modularity of Mind*. Cambridge, MA, MIT Press.

Fodor, J. (2004) 'Water's water everywhere'. *London Review of Books* 26(20):17–19.

Fodor, J. D. (2001) 'Parameters and the periphery: reflections on *Syntactic Nuts*'. *Journal of Linguistics* 37:367–92.

French, R. and M. Jacquet (2004) 'Understanding bilingual memory: models and data'. *Trends in Cognitive Sciences* 8:87–93.

Frith, U. (1991) 'Asperger and his syndrome'. In U. Frith (ed.) *Autism and Asperger Syndrome*. Cambridge, Cambridge University Press, pp. 1–36.

Frith, U. (2003) *Autism: Explaining the Enigma*. 2nd edn. Oxford, Blackwell.

Fromkin, V. (ed.) (2000) *Linguistics: An Introduction to Linguistic Theory*. Oxford, Blackwell.

Fromkin, V., R. Rodman and N. Hyams (2003) *An Introduction to Language*. 7th edn. Boston, Thomson Heinle.

Froud, K. (2001) 'Prepositions and the lexical/functional divide: aphasic evidence'. *Lingua* 111:1–28.

Fudge, E. (1969) 'Syllables'. *Journal of Linguistics* 5:253–86.

Furlow, B. (2001) 'The making of a mind'. *New Scientist* (21 July) 38–41.

Gallagher, S., J. Cole and D. McNeill (2002) 'Social cognition and primacy of movement revisited'. *Trends in Cognitive Sciences* 6:155–6.

Gallese, V., C. Keysers and G. Rizzolatti (2004) 'A unifying view of the basis of social cognition'. *Trends in Cognitive Sciences* 8:396–403.

Garfield, J., C. Peterson and T. Perry (2001) 'Social cognition, language acquisition and the development of theory of mind'. *Mind & Language* 16:494–541.

Gazdar, G., E. Klein, G. K. Pullum and I. Sag (1985) *Generalised Phrase Structure Grammar*. Oxford, Blackwell.

Gelman, R. and C. R. Gallistel (1978) *The Child's Understanding of Number*. Cambridge, MA, Harvard University Press.

Gentner, D. and S. Goldin-Meadow (eds.) (2003) *Language in Mind*. Cambridge, MA, MIT Press.

Giles, H., N. Coupland and J. Coupland (1991) 'Accommodation theory: communication, context, and consequence'. In *Contexts of Accommodation: Developments in Applied Sociolinguistics*. Cambridge, Cambridge University Press, pp. 1–68.

Gilligan, J. (2001) *Preventing Violence*. London, Thames and Hudson.

Gleick, J. (1992) *Genius: Richard Feynman and Modern Physics*. London, Abacus.

Gnanadesikan, A. (1995) 'Markedness and faithfulness constraints in child phonology'. Rutgers Optimality Archive 67; http://ruccs.rutgers.edu/roa.html.

Gopnik, M. and M. Crago (1991) 'Familial aggregation of a developmental language disorder'. *Cognition* 39:1–50.

Grandin, T. (1986) *Emergence: Labeled Autistic*. Novato, CA; Arena Press.

Greenbaum, S. and R. Quirk (1990) *A Student's Grammar of the English Language*. London, Longman.

Groce, N. (1985) *Everyone Here Spoke Sign Language: Hereditary Deafness on Martha's Vineyard*. Cambridge, MA, Harvard University Press.

Gussenhoven, C. (2002) *Phonology: Analysis and Theory*. Cambridge, Cambridge University Press.

Haeberli, E. (2002) 'Analyzing Old and Middle English V2: evidence from the distribution of subjects and adjuncts'. Paper presented at the LAGB, UMIST, September.

Hagan, P. (2004) 'Falling on deaf ears'. *New Scientist* (28 August) 36–9.

Hale, S. (2002) *The Man who Lost his Language*. London, Allen Lane.

Halle, M. (1988) 'The Bloomfield–Jakobson correspondence, 1944–1946'. *Language* 64:737–54.

Happé, F. (1991) 'The autobiographical writings of three Asperger syndrome adults: problems of interpretation and implications for theory'. In U. Frith (ed.) *Autism and Asperger Syndrome*. Cambridge, Cambridge University Press, pp. 207–42.

Happé, F. (1999) 'Autism: cognitive deficit or cognitive style?'. *Trends in Cognitive Sciences* 3(6):216–22.

Harbert, W. (1995) 'Binding theory, control and *pro.*' In G. Webelhuth (ed.) *Government and Binding Theory and the Minimalist Program*. Oxford, Blackwell, pp. 177–240.

Harris, R. A. (1993) *The Linguistics Wars*. New York, Oxford University Press.

Hauser, M., N. Chomsky and W. Tecumseh Fitch (2002) 'The faculty of language: what is it, who has it, and how did it evolve?'. *Science* 298:1569–79.

Hayes, B. (2004) 'Phonological acquisition in Optimality Theory: the early stages'. In R. Kager, J. Pater and W. Zonneveld (eds.) *Constraints in Phonological Acquisition*. Cambridge University Press, pp. 158–203.

Heider, F. and M. Simmel (1944) 'An experimental study of apparent behavior'. *American Journal of Psychology* 57:243–59.

Heim, I. and A. Kratzer (1998) *Semantics in Generative Grammar*. Oxford, Blackwell.

Hermelin, B. (2001) *Bright Splinters of the Mind: A Personal Story of Research with Autistic Savants*. London, Jessica Kingsley.

Hill, E. (2004) 'Executive dysfunction in autism'. *Trends in Cognitive Sciences* 8:26–32.

Holmberg, A. and G. Sandström (1996) 'Scandinavian possessive constructions from a Northern Swedish viewpoint'. In J. Black and V. Motapanyane (eds.) *Microparametric Syntax and Dialect Variation*. Amsterdam, John Benjamins, pp. 95–120.

Hornstein, N. (1990) *As Time Goes By: Tense and Universal Grammar*. Cambridge, MA, MIT Press.

Huddleston, R. and G. K. Pullum (2002) *The Cambridge Grammar of English*. Cambridge, Cambridge University Press.

Hudson, R. A. (1990) *English Word Grammar*. Oxford, Blackwell.

Hudson, R. A. (1996) *Sociolinguistics*. 2nd edn. Cambridge, Cambridge University Press.

Hudson, R. A. (2001) 'Clitics in word grammar'. *UCL Working Papers in Linguistics* 13:243–94.

Hyams, N. (1986) *Language Acquisition and the Theory of Parameters.* Dordrecht, Reidel.

Hyams, N. (1996) 'The underspecification of functional categories in early grammar'. In H. Clahsen (ed.) *Generative Perspectives on Language Acquisition.* Amsterdam, John Benjamins, pp. 91–127.

Ingram, D. (1974) 'Phonological rules in young children'. *Journal of Child Language* 1:49–64.

Ingram, J. and H. Chenery (in prep.) *Language Processing in the Human Brain.* Cambridge, Cambridge University Press.

Ivic, M. (1965) *Trends in Linguistics.* The Hague, Mouton.

Jackendoff, R. (2002) *Foundations of Language: Brain, Meaning, Grammar, Evolution.* Oxford, Oxford University Press.

Janse, M. and S. Tol (eds.) (2003) *Language Death and Language Maintenance: Theoretical, Practical and Descriptive Approaches.* Amsterdam: John Benjamins.

Jenkins, L. (2000) *Biolinguistics: Exploring the Biology of Language.* Cambridge, Cambridge University Press.

Jusczyk, P. (1997) *The Discovery of Spoken Language.* Cambridge, MA, MIT Press.

Kang, H.-K. (2001) 'Quantifier spreading: linguistic and pragmatic considerations'. *Lingua* 111:591–627.

Kang, H.-K. (2002) *Aspects of the Acquisition of Quantification: Experimental Studies of English and Korean Children.* Seoul, Hankook.

Kaplan, M. (2004) 'Save the rhino maggot!'. *New Scientist* (27 March) 40–3.

Karmiloff, K. and A. Karmiloff-Smith (2001) *Pathways to Language: From Fetus to Adolescent.* Cambridge, MA, Harvard University Press.

Karmiloff-Smith, A. (1994) *Baby it's You.* London, Ebury Press.

Karmiloff-Smith, A. (1998) 'Development itself is the key to understanding developmental disorders'. *Trends in Cognitive Sciences* 2:389–98.

Kent, R. (1992) 'The biology of phonological development'. In C. Ferguson, L. Menn and C. Stoel-Gammon (eds.) *Phonological Development: Models, Research, Implications.* Timonium, MD, York Press, pp. 65–90.

Kermode, F. (2000) *Shakespeare's Language.* London, Penguin.

Kiparsky, V. (1952) *L'histoire du morse.* Helsinki. (Annales Academiae Scientiarum Fennicae. Ser. B, 73:3.)

Kiparsky, V. (1979) *Russian Historical Grammar.* Ann Arbor, Ardis.

Klin, A. (2000) 'Attributing social meaning to ambiguous visual stimuli in higher-functioning autism and Asperger syndrome: the Social Attribution Task'. *Journal of Child Psychology and Psychiatry* 7:831–46.

Krauss, M. (1992) 'The world's languages in crisis'. *Language* 68:4–10.

Kroch, A. (1989) 'Function and grammar in the history of English periphrastic *do*'. In R. Fasold and D. Schiffrin (eds.) *Language Variation and Change.* Philadelphia, John Benjamins, pp. 199–244.

Kroch, A. (2002) 'Variation and change in the historical syntax of English'. Paper presented at the LAGB, UMIST, September.

Kuhn, T. S. (1970) *The Structure of Scientific Revolutions*. Chicago, University of Chicago Press.

Lakatos, I. (1970) 'Falsification and the methodology of scientific research programmes'. In I. Lakatos and A. Musgrave (eds.) *Criticism and the Growth of Knowledge*. Cambridge, Cambridge University Press, pp. 91–195.

Landau, I. (2000) *Elements of Control: Structure and Meaning in Infinitival Constructions*. Dordrecht, Kluwer.

Law, A. (2004) 'Sentence-final focus particles in Cantonese'. PhD thesis, University College London.

Leroi, A. (2003) *Mutants: On the Form, Varieties and Errors of the Human Body*. London, HarperCollins.

Leslie, A. (1988) 'The necessity of illusion'. In L. Weiskrantz (ed.) *Thought without Language*. Oxford; Clarendon Press, pp. 185–210.

Leslie, A., O. Friedman and T. German (2004) 'Core mechanisms in "theory of mind"'. *Trends in Cognitive Sciences* 8:528–33.

Lidz, J. and L. Gleitman (2004) 'Argument structure and the child's contribution to language learning'. *Trends in Cognitive Sciences* 8:157–61.

Lieberman, P. (2000) *Human Language and our Reptilian Brain: The Subcortical Bases of Speech, Syntax and Thought*. Cambridge, MA, Harvard University Press.

Lieberman, P. (2001) 'On the subcortical bases of the evolution of language'. In J. Trabant and S. Ward (eds.) *New Essays on the Origin of Language*. Berlin, Mouton de Gruyter, pp. 21–40.

Lightfoot, D. (1999) *The Development of Language: Acquisition, Change, and Evolution*. Oxford, Blackwell.

Lindblom, B. (1992) 'Phonological units as adaptive emergents of lexical development'. In C. Ferguson, L. Menn and C. Stoel-Gammon (eds.) *Phonological Development: Models, Research, Implications*. Timonium, MD, York Press, pp. 131–63.

Love, T. and D. Swinney (1996) 'Antecedent reactivation demonstrated by cross-modal priming'. *Journal of Psycholinguistic Research*, 25:5–24.

Macken, M. (1980) 'The child's lexical representation: the *puzzle–puddle–pickle* evidence'. *Journal of Linguistics* 16:1–17.

Majid, A., M. Bowerman, S. Kita, D. Haun and S. Levinson (2004) 'Can language restructure cognition? The case for space'. *Trends in Cognitive Sciences* 8:108–14.

Marcus, G. and S. Fisher (2003) 'FOXP2 in focus: what can genes tell us about speech and language?'. *Trends in Cognitive Sciences* 7:257–62.

Marks, P. (2002) 'Texts that trigger meltdown'. *New Scientist* (7 September) 12–13.

Masataka, N. (1998) 'Perception of motherese in Japanese Sign Language by 6-month-old hearing infants'. *Developmental Psychology* 34:241–6.

McGilvray, J. (1999) *Chomsky: Language, Mind, and Politics*. Cambridge, Polity.

McGilvray, J. (ed.) (2005) *The Cambridge Companion to Chomsky*. Cambridge, Cambridge University Press.

Menn, L. and E. Matthei (1992) 'The "two-lexicon" account of child phonology: looking back, looking ahead'. In C. Ferguson, L. Menn and C. Stoel-Gammon (eds.) *Phonological Development: Models, Research, Implications*. Timonium, MD, York Press, pp. 211–47.

Miller, P. (1997) 'Les morphèmes zéro à l'épreuve du rasoir d'Occam'. In G. Deléchelle and M. Fryd (eds.) *Travaux Linguistiques du CERLICO* 10:13–42. Presses Universitaires de Rennes.

Milloy, J. (1999) 'When a language dies'. *Index on Censorship* 28(4):54–64. [This issue of *Index* has a numbing catalogue of assaults on minority languages.]

Morgan, G., N. Smith, I.-M. Tsimpli and B. Woll (2002) 'Language against the odds: the learning of British Sign Language by a polyglot savant'. *Journal of Linguistics* 38:1–41.

Morgan, G., N. Smith, I.-M. Tsimpli and B. Woll (in prep.) *The Signs of a Savant*. Cambridge, Cambridge University Press.

Morton, J. and N. V. Smith (1974) 'Some ideas concerning the acquisition of phonology' In F. Bresson (ed.) *Problèmes Actuels en Psycholinguistique*. Paris, CNRS, pp. 161–77.

Neeleman, A. and F. Weerman (1997) 'L1 and L2 word order acquisition'. *Language Acquisition* 6:125–70.

Neidle, C., J. Kegl, D. MacLaughlin, B. Bahan and R. Lee (2000). *The Syntax of American Sign Language: Functional Categories and Hierarchical Structure*. Cambridge, MA, MIT Press.

Newbury, D. F. and A. P. Monaco (2002) 'Molecular genetics of speech and language disorders'. *Current Opinion in Pediatrics* 14:696–701.

Newmeyer, F. (1980) *Linguistic Theory in America: The First Quarter-Century of Transformational Generative Grammar*. New York, Academic Press.

Newport, E. and R. Meier (1985) 'The acquisition of American Sign Language'. In Đ. Slobin (ed.) *The Cross-Linguistic Study of Language Acquisition. Vol. 1: The Data*. Hillsdale, NJ, Lawrence Erlbaum, pp. 881–938.

Nicoladis, E., R. Mayberry and F. Genesee (1999) 'Gesture and early bilingual development'. *Developmental Psychology* 35:514–26.

Nowak, M. and N. Komarova (2001) 'Towards an evolutionary theory of language'. *Trends in Cognitive Sciences* 5:288–95.

Nurmi, E., M. Dowd, O. Tadevosyan-Leyfer, J. Haines, S. Folstein and J. Sutcliffe (2003) 'Exploratory subsetting of autism families based on savant skills improves evidence of genetic linkage to 15q11-q13'. *Journal of the American Academy of Child and Adolescent Psychiatry* 42:856–63.

O'Connor, N. and B. Hermelin (1989) 'The memory structure of autistic idiot-savant mnemonists'. *British Journal of Psychology*, 80:97–111.

Ogden, C. K. (1940) *Basic English: A General Introduction with Rules and Grammar*. 8th edn. London, Kegan Paul.

Onishi, K. and R. Baillargeon (submitted) '15-month-old infants understand false beliefs'.

Papafragou, A. (1998) 'The acquisition of modality: implications for theories of semantic representation'. *Mind & Language* 13:370–99.

Papafragou, A. (2002) 'Mindreading and verbal communication'. *Mind & Language* 17:55–67.

Patel, A. (2003) 'Language, music, syntax and the brain'. *Nature Neuroscience* 6:674–81.

Peck, J. (1987) *The Chomsky Reader*. New York, Pantheon.

Pepperberg, I. (2002) 'Who's a clever boy then?'. *Trends in Cognitive Sciences* 6:154 [report by H. Johansen-Berg].

Petitto, L. A. (1999). 'The acquisition of natural signed languages: lessons in the nature of human language and its biological foundations'. In C. Chamberlain, J. Morford and R. Mayberry (eds.) *Language Acquisition by Eye*. Mahwah, NJ, Lawrence Erlbaum, pp. 41–50.

Petitto, L. A., S. Holowka, L. Sergio and D. Ostry (2001) 'Language rhythms in babies' hand movements'. *Nature* 413:35–6.

Pickering, M. and G. Barry (1991) 'Sentence processing without empty categories'. *Language and Cognitive Processes* 6:229–59.

Pintzuk, S. (2002) 'Objects in Old English: why Early English isn't Icelandic'. Paper presented at the LAGB, UMIST, September.

Postal, P. (in press) *Skeptical Linguistic Essays*.

Postal, P. and G. K. Pullum (1982) 'The contraction debate'. *Linguistic Inquiry* 13:122–38.

Pullum, G. K. (1997) 'The morpholexical nature of *to*-contraction'. *Language* 73:79–102.

Pullum, G. K. and A. Zwicky (1988) 'The syntax–phonology interface.' In F. Newmeyer (ed.) *Linguistics: The Cambridge Survey*. Cambridge, Cambridge University Press, vol. I:255–80.

Pullum, G. K. and A. Zwicky (1992) 'A misconceived approach to morphology'. *WCCFL (West Coast Conference on Formal Linguistics)* 10:387–98.

Radford, A. (1990) *Syntactic Theory and the Acquisition of English Syntax*. Oxford, Blackwell.

Radford, A. (2004a) *English Syntax: An Introduction*. Cambridge, Cambridge University Press.

Radford, A. (2004b) *Minimalist Syntax: Exploring the Structure of English*. Cambridge, Cambridge University Press.

Ramus, F., S. Rosen, S. Dakin, et al. (2003) 'Theories of developmental dyslexia: Insights from a multiple case study of dyslexic adults'. *Brain* 126:841–65.

Reichenbach, H. (1947) *Elements of Symbolic Logic*. New York, Free Press.

Reinhart, T. and E. Reuland (1993) 'Reflexivity'. *Linguistic Inquiry* 24:657–720.

Rieffe, C. and M. M. Terwogt (2000) 'Deaf children's understanding of emotions: desire takes precedence'. *Journal of Child Psychology and Psychiatry* 41:601–8.

Rizzi, L. (2002) 'On the grammatical basis of language development: a case study'. University of Siena. http://www.ciscl.unisi.it/doc/doc_pub/rizzi2002-on_the_grammatical_basis_of_language_development.doc

Robinson, A. (2002) 'A grouse for Mr Bigwiz'. *Times Higher Educational Supplement* (9 August).

Roca, I. and W. Johnson (1999) *A Course in Phonology*. Oxford, Blackwell.

Roeper, T. (2000) 'Inherent binding and the syntax/lexicon interface: distinguishing DP, NP, and N'. In P. Coopmans, M. Everaert and J. Grimshaw (eds.) *Lexical Specification and Insertion*, Amsterdam and Philadelphia, John Benjamins, pp. 305–28.

Rooryck, J. (2001) 'Evidentiality'. *Glot International* 5:125–33.

Ross, A. S. C. (1952) *Ginger: A Loan-Word Study*. Oxford, Blackwell.

Russell, B. (1905) 'On denoting'. *Mind* 14:479–93.

Saffran, J., E. Newport and R. Aslin (1996) 'Statistical learning by eight-month-old infants'. *Science* 274:1926–8.

Sampson, G. (1999) *Educating Eve: The 'Language Instinct' Debate*. London, Cassell.

Samuels, R. (2004) 'Innateness in cognitive science'. *Trends in Cognitive Sciences* 8:136–41.

Schmaling, C. (2000) *Maganar Hannu: Language of the Hands. A Descriptive Analysis of Hausa Sign Language. International Studies on Sign Language and Communication of the Deaf. Vol. 35.* Hamburg, Signum Verlag.

Schütze, C. (1996) *The Empirical Base of Linguistics: Grammaticality Judgments and Linguistic Methodology*. Chicago, University of Chicago Press.

Sloboda, J., B. Hermelin and N. O'Connor (1985) 'An exceptional musical memory'. *Music Perception* 3:155–70.

Smith, N. V. (1967) *An Outline Grammar of Nupe*. London, SOAS.

Smith, N. V. (1973) *The Acquisition of Phonology: A Case Study*. Cambridge, Cambridge University Press.

Smith, N. V. (1989a) *The Twitter Machine: Reflections on Language*. Oxford, Blackwell.

Smith, N. V. (1989b) 'Must and the randy pachyderm'. In *The Twitter Machine*. Oxford, Blackwell, pp. 83–93.

Smith, N. V. (1994) 'Competence and performance.' In the *Pergamon Encyclopaedia of Linguistics*. Oxford, Pergamon, vol. 2:645–48.

Smith, N. V. (1997) 'Structural eccentricities'. *Glot International* 2(8):7. [Reprinted in *Language, Bananas and Bonobos: Linguistic Problems, Puzzles and Polemics*. Oxford, Blackwell, pp. 110–15.]

Smith, N. V. (1998a) 'Jackdaws, sex and language acquisition'. *Glot International*. 3(7):7. [Reprinted in *Language, Bananas and Bonobos: Linguistic Problems, Puzzles and Polemics*. Oxford, Blackwell, pp. 95–9.]

Smith, N. V. (1998b) 'Dissociations'. *Glot International* 3(9/10):10. [Reprinted in *Language, Bananas and Bonobos: Linguistic Problems, Puzzles and Polemics*. Oxford, Blackwell, pp. 40–5.]

Smith, N. V. (1999) 'The velarity of linguists'. *Glot International* 4(1):10. [Reprinted in *Language, Bananas and Bonobos: Linguistic Problems, Puzzles and Polemics*. Oxford, Blackwell, pp. 116–20.]

Smith, N. V. (2001) 'Truth in the silence of mushrooms'. *Times Higher Educational Supplement* (9 February).

Smith, N. V. (2002) *Language, Bananas and Bonobos: Linguistic Problems, Puzzles and Polemics*. Oxford, Blackwell.

Smith, N. V. (2003a) 'Dissociation and modularity: reflections on language and mind'. In M. Banich and M. Mack (eds.) *Mind, Brain and Language*. Mahwah, NJ, Lawrence Erlbaum, pp. 87–111.

Smith, N. V. (2003b) 'Representations and responsibilities'. *Korean Journal of English Language and Linguistics* 3:527–45.

Smith, N. V. (2004) *Chomsky: Ideas and Ideals*. 2nd edn. Cambridge, Cambridge University Press. [Originally published 1999.]

Smith, N. V. and A. Smith (1988) 'A relevance-theoretic account of conditionals'. In L. Hyman and C. Li (eds.) *Language, Speech and Mind: Studies in Honor of Victoria A. Fromkin*. London, Routledge, pp. 322–52.

Smith, N. V. and I.-M. Tsimpli (1995) *The Mind of a Savant: Language-Learning and Modularity*. Oxford, Blackwell.

Smith, N. V. and I.-M. Tsimpli (1996) 'Putting a banana in your ear'. *Glot International* 2(1/2):28. [Reprinted in *Language, Bananas and Bonobos: Linguistic Problems, Puzzles and Polemics*. Oxford, Blackwell, pp. 18–23.]

Smith, N. V., B. Hermelin and I.-M. Tsimpli (2003) 'Dissociation of social affect and theory of mind in a case of Asperger syndrome'. *UCL Working Papers in Linguistics* 15:357–77.

Smolensky, P. (1996) 'On the comprehension/production dilemma in child language'. *Linguistic Inquiry* 27:720–31.

Soja, N., S. Carey and E. Spelke (1991) 'Ontological categories guide young children's inductions of word meaning: object terms and substance terms'. *Cognition* 38:179–211.

Sokal, A. (1996a) 'Transgressing the boundaries: toward a transformative hermeneutics of quantum gravity'. *Social Text* 46–7:217–52.

Sokal, A. (1996b) 'A physicist experiments with cultural studies'. *Lingua Franca* (May/June) 62–4.

Spelke, E. and S. Tsivkin (2001) 'Initial knowledge and conceptual change: space and number'. In M. Bowerman and S. Levinson (eds.) *Language Acquisition and Conceptual Development*. Cambridge, Cambridge University Press, pp. 70–97.

Spelke, E., K. Breinliger, J. Macomber and K. Jacobson (1992) 'Origins of knowledge'. *Psychological Review* 99:605–32.

Sperber, D. and D. Wilson (1995) *Relevance: Communication and Cognition*. 2nd edn. Oxford, Blackwell.

Stampe, D. (1969) 'The acquisition of phonetic representation'. In R. Binnick, A. Davidson, G. Green and J. Morgan (eds.) *Papers from the Fifth Regional Meeting, Chicago Linguistics Society*. Chicago, Chicago Linguistics Society, pp. 433–44.

Steiner, G. (1998) *After Babel*. 3rd edn. Oxford, Oxford University Press.

Stemberger, J. (1992) 'A connectionist view of child phonology: phonological processing without phonological processes'. In C. Ferguson, L. Menn and C. Stoel-Gammon (eds.) *Phonological Development: Models, Research, Implications*. Timonium, MD, York Press, pp. 165–89.

Stojanovik, V., M. Perkins and S. Howard (2004) 'Williams syndrome and specific language impairment do not support claims for developmental double dissociation and innate modularity'. *Journal of Neurolinguistics* 17:403–24.

Stokoe, W. (1960) *Sign Language Structure: An Outline of the Visual Communication System of the American Deaf*. Buffalo, NY, University of Buffalo.

Sweetser, E. (1990) *From Etymology to Pragmatics: Metaphorical and Cultural Aspects of Semantic Structure*. Cambridge, Cambridge University Press.

Swinney, D. and L. Osterhout (1990) 'Inference generation during auditory language comprehension'. In A. Graesser and G. Bower (eds.) *The Psychology of Learning and Motivation*. New York, Academic Press, vol. 25:17–33.

Tang, C.-C. J. (2001) 'Functional projections and adverbial expressions in Chinese'. *Language and Linguistics* 2(2):203–41.

Tang, T.-C. (1992) 'The syntax and semantics of resultative complements in Chinese: a comparative study of Mandarin and Southern Min'. In T.-C. Tang (ed.) *Studies in Chinese Morphology and Syntax*. Taipei, Student Book Co., vol. 4:165–204.

Tantam, D. (1991) 'Asperger syndrome in adulthood'. In U. Frith (ed.) *Autism and Asperger Syndrome*. Cambridge, Cambridge University Press, pp. 147–83.

Tesar, B. and P. Smolensky (2000) *Learnability in Optimality Theory*. Cambridge, MA, MIT Press.

Tomasello, M. (1999) *The Cultural Origins of Human Cognition*. Cambridge, MA, Harvard University Press.

Tomasello, M. (2000a) 'Do young children have adult syntactic competence?'. *Cognition* 74:209–53.

Tomasello, M. (2000b) 'The item-based nature of children's early syntactic development'. *Trends in Cognitive Sciences* 4:156–63.

Traugott, E. and R. Dasher (2002) *Regularity in Semantic Change*. Cambridge, Cambridge University Press.

Treffert, D. (1989) *Extraordinary People*. London, Bantam.

Tsimpli, I.-M. and N. Smith (1993) 'LF and post-LF in a polyglot *savant's* grammars'. *Newcastle and Durham Working Papers in Linguistics* 1:276–91.

Tsimpli, I.-M. and N. V. Smith (1998) 'Modules and quasi-modules'. *Learning and Individual Differences* 10:193–215.

Ullmann, S. (1959) *The Principles of Semantics*. Oxford, Blackwell.

Van der Berghe, P. L. (1983) 'Human inbreeding avoidance: culture in nature'. *Behavioral and Brain Sciences* 6:91–123.

Van der Lely, H. (1998) 'SLI in children: movement, economy and deficits in the syntactic-computational system'. *Language Acquisition* 72:161–92.

Van Kampen, J. (2004) 'An acquisitional view on optionality'. *Lingua* 114:1133–46.

Vihman, M. (1996) *Phonological Development: The Origins of Language in the Child*. Oxford, Blackwell.

Vikner, C. and S. Vikner (1997) 'The aspectual complexity of the simple past in English: a comparison with French and Danish'. In C. Bache and A. Klinge (eds.) *Sounds, Structures and Senses: Essays Presented to Niels Davidsen-Nielsen on the Occasion of his Sixtieth Birthday*. Odense: Odense University Press, pp. 267–84.

Vikner, S. (1995) *Verb Movement and Expletive Subjects in the Germanic Languages*. Oxford Studies in Comparative Syntax. New York, Oxford University Press.

Wellman, H. (1990) *The Child's Theory of Mind*. Cambridge, MA, MIT Press.

Whorf, B. L. (1941) 'The relation of habitual thought and behavior to language'. In L. Spier (ed.) *Language, Culture, and Personality: Essays in Memory of Edward Sapir*. Menasha, WI, Sapir Memorial Publication Fund, pp. 75–93.

Wiese, H. (2003) *Numbers, Language and the Human Mind*. Cambridge, Cambridge University Press.

Willey, L. (1999) *Pretending to be Normal*. London, Jessica Kingsley.

Williams, D. (1992) *Nobody Nowhere*. London, Doubleday.

Williams, D. (1994) *Somebody Somewhere*. London, Doubleday.

Williams, D. (1996) *Like Color to the Blind*. New York, Random House.

Wing, L. (1991) 'The relationship between Asperger's syndrome and Kanner's autism'. In U. Frith (ed.) *Autism and Asperger Syndrome*. Cambridge, Cambridge University Press, pp. 93–121.

Winston, M. (2002) *On Chomsky*. Wadsworth Philosophers Series. Belmont, CA, Wadsworth/Thomson Learning.

Wolpert, L. (1992) *The Unnatural Nature of Science*. London, Faber and Faber.

Wolpert, L. (2002) Interview in *Camden New Journal* (22 August). London.

Wynn, K. (1998) 'Psychological foundations of number: numerical competence in human infants'. *Trends in Cognitive Sciences* 2:296–303.

Yang, C. (2004) 'Universal Grammar, statistics or both?'. *Trends in Cognitive Sciences* 8:451–6.

Yip, M. (2003) 'Casting doubt on the Onset–Rime distinction'. *Lingua* 113:779–816.

Index

Items in **bold type** have an entry in the glossary (pp. 159ff).